Behavioural Res

Marketing

This book, the first of its kind, provides market researchers and marketeers with the tools to better understand human behaviour by drawing upon social science theory from different schools of thought, including sociology, psychology and behavioural economics. It has practical examples throughout to help illustrate how to operationalise theory in market research and to underpin the way we understand how people think, behave, decide and make choices. Each theory is explained in accessible terms to ensure that the content is relevant and useful to commercial market researchers.

By considering different theoretical models of human behaviour from the outset, this book will open new avenues of investigation, help researchers to develop more dynamic and challenging hypotheses to test during the research process, and ultimately result in more insightful outcomes. The book brings together theories that look at how society is shaped and formed, and how this impacts on the individual, along with theories that focus on the mind and behaviour of the individual; these perspectives are equally important in market research but not usually considered within the same text. This book is not limited to theory alone; in each chapter, illustrative examples are used to help demonstrate how theory can be applied to real-world market research projects. Additionally, throughout there are helpful suggestions in terms of question content to help operationalise theory.

This book will appeal to those that have recently entered the field of market research and are interested in the theoretical underpinnings of human behaviour, undergraduates and post-graduates that are studying marketing, business studies or social science, where a core component of the course requirement is market research, and finally those that are users of market research data and want a working knowledge of key theories of human behaviour.

Julian Adams has worked in the market research industry for over 20 years. He is a Director at Motif, a brand, CX and loyalty insights agency. Prior to this, he was a Partner at Illuminas LLP. Julian is a guest lecturer at Kingston University Business School, where he teaches research theory, method and nonverbal communication.

Behavioural Research for Marketing

A Practitioner's Handbook

Julian Adams

Routledge
Taylor & Francis Group

LONDON AND NEW YORK

Cover image: Getty/filo

First published 2023
by Routledge
4 Park Square, Milton Park, Abingdon, Oxon OX14 4RN

and by Routledge
605 Third Avenue, New York, NY 10158

Routledge is an imprint of the Taylor & Francis Group, an informa business

British Library Cataloguing-in-Publication Data
A catalogue record for this book is available from the British Library

Library of Congress Cataloging-in-Publication Data
A catalog record has been requested for this book

ISBN: 978-0-367-77131-7 (hbk)
ISBN: 978-0-367-77133-1 (pbk)
ISBN: 978-1-003-16993-2 (ebk)

DOI: 10.4324/9781003169932

Typeset in Adobe Garamond Pro
by codeMantra

Contents

This book is aimed at those who are intellectually curious, those looking to go beyond reportage and seek explanations for human behaviour bounded by theory. Against this context, this book will appeal to the following audiences:

- Individuals that have recently entered the field of market research and are interested in the theoretical underpinnings of human behaviour.
- Undergraduates and post-graduates that are studying marketing, business studies or social science, where a core component of the course requirement is market research.
- Those that are users of market research data and want a working knowledge of key theories of human behaviour.

Acknowledgements

This book is dedicated to my wonderful partner Claire, who has been steadfast in her support and encouragement throughout. I am truly grateful to Gavin Mulholland for his patience, support and invaluable guidance in helping me shape an idea into a book. I would like to thank friends, family and colleagues, who politely endured my often-impassioned diatribes about the vision and content of this book. Finally, my thanks must go out to the team at Routledge without whom this book would not have seen the light of day.

Chapter 1

Introducing theory

CHAPTER OVERVIEW

1.1 We begin by considering the role of theory and how theory informs research from connecting researchers to a body of knowledge through to the implementation of findings.

1.2 Next, how philosophical perspectives shape the nature of theory is discussed.

1.3 In the final part of this opening chapter, the overall aim and content of the book are presented.

Introduction

Before reviewing theories of human behaviour, the nature and role of theory in behavioural research must be considered. Further, no discussion about theory would be complete without considering the research philosophies that sit behind theory. Research philosophies make existential assumptions about how we experience and accrue knowledge about social reality. Although this might seem a little abstract, research philosophies are instrumental in the development and application of theory in social science.

DOI: 10.4324/9781003169932-1

1.1 Applying theory as a research decision tool

1.1.1 Defining theory

Commonly, theory is defined as a way in which to explain observed patterns of behaviour in relation to a given event or circumstance. Even with this definition in mind, theory might seem somewhat indeterminate. Alternatively, if we consider theory as a research decision tool, the nature and purpose of theory become clearer. Theory helps inform decisions throughout the research process, from introducing researchers to a body of knowledge, through to making recommendations and implementation. The role of theory throughout the research process is detailed in Figure 1.1.

1.1.2 How theory evolves over time

Theory is not constant, but dynamic and evolving: over time, new research is conducted, and consequently, new data is created. New data is interpreted resulting

Theory as a primer to research

- Theory helps to connect researchers to existing knowledge within the domain of the research problem.
- Theory allows researchers to identify gaps / omissions in knowledge.
- Without theory, the process of research would be hugely inefficient, as researchers would be starting from a blank slate each time.

Theory as a behavioural predictor

- Theory permits researchers to make predictions about behaviour with a degree of confidence.
- Theory provides guidance on the relationship between factors / variables.
- There are likely to be many interrelationships between factors / variables, theory helps focus resources on factors / variables that are pursuant to the research problem. In turn, this will ensure that researchers can formulate hypotheses to test.

Theory as a methodological system

- Theory helps to inform the design and execution of research.
- Theory provides pointers in terms of what might constitute the optimum method and data collection technique.

Theory as an interpretative lens

- In absence of theory, data is dumb, it confers no obvious value, it is only through interpretation does data come to mean something.
- Reviewing data through the lens of theory helps give saliency and perspective. That is, rather than research existing in isolation, theory provides a framework in which to interpret data.

Theory as a means to generalise findings

- Without theory, researchers are limited to simply describing findings.
- Theory helps researchers address how, why and where? In so doing, researchers can make informed decisions about the generalisability of research findings.

Theory as a means of implementation

- The implementation of research findings is not undertaken in a theoretical vacuum, but is driven by the working principles of theory that first informed the research.

Figure 1.1 Theory as a decision tool

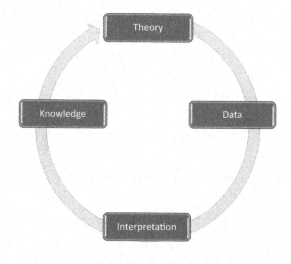

Figure 1.2 The knowledge cycle of theory

in new knowledge. New knowledge serves to give weight to theory, refute existing theoretical assumptions, or provide a new perspective on theory. In turn, theory evolves to accommodate new knowledge which will pose new hypotheses to test, and the research cycle continues as illustrated in Figure 1.2.

1.1.3 Connecting researchers to theory

In academia, researchers will conduct a literature review of theory prior to engaging in primary research; this involves looking at relevant books and research journals to locate theory to help address the research problem at hand. In market research, theory is more nuanced; as in the academic world, research practitioners might conduct a literature review but also draw upon what is known within the company that is commissioning the research or the research agency that is going to conduct the research, to identify any assumptions/running hypotheses that exist. Researchers might also talk to industry experts to help shed light on the macro issues pertaining to the research problem. The net result is a body of knowledge that could be loosely referred to as theory. Irrespective of the nature of research, theory is at the very heart of what researchers do.

1.1.4 Determining theory prediction and testability

In social science, there are broadly three categories of theory: grand, middle-range and micro theories, with varying degrees of predictability and testability, as illustrated in Figure 1.3.

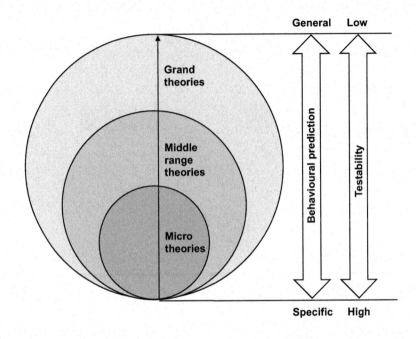

Figure 1.3 Grand, middle and micro theory prediction and testability

1.1.4.1 *Defining grand theories*

Grand theories were in the ascendancy in the mid-20th century. Typically, these theories make gross generalisations about society and behaviour. Functionalism is a grand theory of sociology that suggests there are social systems that function to ensure that in society there is solidarity and stability. Cognitivism is a grand theory of psychology that uses cognitive models to explain information processing that occurs in the human mind. Given grand theories make broad statements about society and behaviour, they can seem a little fuzzy and consequently difficult to confirm or refute in practise. However, grand theories have stood the test of time, by virtue of offering the researcher different perspectives in which to interpret human behaviour at a meta-level.

1.1.4.2 *Defining middle-range theories*

Middle-range (or emerging) theories are less abstract than grand theories but are sufficiently general to be applied to different social behaviours. These theories can be tested and as such, can be confirmed or refuted in practise. Today, middle-range theories are common in social science.

1.1.4.3 *Defining micro theories*

Micro theories look at behaviour in specific situations/settings. These theories are not suitable for making gross generalisations about behaviour, given the specificity of the theory. Such theories might be better understood as a series of hypotheses/ assumptions, rather than a unified theory *per se*. In market research, whilst there might not be an 'off-the-shelf' theory to hand, there are likely to be running hypotheses that exist, that can be brought to bear on the research. Hypotheses can be explicitly tested and accepted or rejected based on data.

1.2 How research philosophies inform theory

1.2.1 Ontological and epistemology assumptions

Research philosophies make broad assumptions about how we experience and accrue knowledge about social reality. These assumptions help shape and define theory. Specifically, research philosophies make ontological and epistemological assumptions about the social world, as detailed below:

■ Ontology refers to assumptions we make about how we experience reality in the social world.
■ Epistemology refers to assumptions we make about how we create knowledge about the social world.

Ontological assumptions are inextricably linked to epistemological assumptions. For example, if we adopt an ontological assumption that social reality exists external to social actors, then we will logically adopt an epistemological position that human behaviour can be observed based on the laws of experimental science.

1.2.2 Methodological considerations

Epistemological assumptions have implications regarding methodological considerations and data collection. For example, if we follow the laws of experimental science, then a quantitative approach using large-scale surveys will be favoured. Alternatively, if we follow the laws of humanistic theory, then a qualitative approach using groups or in-depth interviews will be favoured.

1.2.3 Research paradigms/frameworks

Together, philosophical assumptions and methodological considerations inform the research framework. A framework consists of the key component of the research process. A framework is sometimes called a research paradigm; the phrase was first coined by the American physicist and philosopher Thomas Kuhn, in his book *The Structure of Scientific Revolutions* (1962). Kuhn argued that in the field of science, over time, we witness paradigm shifts. The phrase is overused and consequently much maligned. That said, the premise is that as anomalies appear that challenge assumptions and established findings of the theoretical doctrine of the day, a new paradigm emerges, resulting in a paradigm shift.

Intriguingly, in social science there is no dominant paradigm, rather, a set of competing paradigms, which can be broadly categorised as follows:

- Objectivism.
- Critical realism.
- Subjectivism.
- Pragmatism.

For each paradigm, it is possible to map out the philosophical assumptions and methodological considerations along with the data collection techniques, as illustrated in Table 1.1.

Although there is no dominant paradigm in social science, objectivism and subjectivism are considered the major paradigms. To illustrate this point, let us look at a couple of psychology theories that subscribe to an objectivist and subjectivist position:

- Behaviourism assumes that we learn behaviour through interactions with our environment. Therefore, the unit of analysis is stimulus in the environment. This deterministic approach places behaviourism within the objectivist research philosophy, where reality is assumed to exist external to the individual and the focus is on the laws of experimental science.
- Maslow's hierarchy of needs theory proposes that there is an order of needs ranging from basic physiological needs extending to higher-order needs about self-esteem and self-actualisation. The theory is based on the existential assumption that we have free will and seek fulfilment in our lives. Therefore, the unit analysis is the social actor. This places the theory within the subjectivist research philosophy, where we look at reality through the lens of the social actor and follow the laws of humanistic theory.

1.2.4 Theory of social structure and individual agency

In social science, many theories have their origins in sociology or psychology. Sociologists look at how societal structures are shaped and formed and for our

Table 1.1 Research philosophy, methodological considerations and data collection

Paradigms/ Research framework	Objectivism	Critical realism	Subjectivism	Pragmatism
Ontology	• Reality exists external to social actors. • We experience reality in the same way, irrespective of our behaviour.	• Reality is socially constructed and under constant societal influence.	• Reality is construed based on our perceptions and actions in the social world.	• View of reality is based on what best addresses the research question.
Epistemology	• Studying social trends in society. • Following the laws of experimental science.	• Studying causation based on power and influence in society. • Following the laws of society.	• Studying social actors. • Following the laws of humanistic theory, looking at the world through the individual's lens.	• Studying social actors and social trends in society. • Focus on practically applied research and integrating perspectives.
Method	• Quantitative techniques. • Analysis to identify facts that imply behavioural rules.	• Ideological review. • Analysis to identify mechanisms that explain behaviour.	• Qualitative techniques. • Analysis to ascertain the subjective meaning of things.	• Range of methods. • Analysis to understand the subjective and objective meaning of things.
Data collection	• Large-scale experimental/ survey.	• Mixed methods. • Archival and historical analysis.	• Small-scale in-depth analysis/ethnography.	• Mixed and multiple methods.

purposes, how this impacts the individual. Psychologists focus on the mind and behaviour of the individual, albeit there is considerable cross-over with sociology and social psychology. In sociology, there is much debate about the primacy and relationship between social structures and individual agency in accounting for human behaviour (the key protagonists are Antony Giddens and Margaret Archer). Giddens (1984) argues that societal structures and individual agency are inseparable, whereby societal structures influence individual behaviour and individuals enact change in the social structures they inhabit. Giddens referred to this recursive relationship between structure and agency as a duality of structure (we return to this notion when we review social practice theory in Section 2.6). From a critical realist position, Archer (1995) argues that the duality results in conflation, where individual agency is reduced to structure and vice versa, thus limiting the researcher's ability to study the relative influence of social structure and individual agency. Whilst acknowledging that structure influences agency, Archer suggests that structure and agency are distinct and operate based on the principle of emergence over time, where structures of the past influence individual behaviour, which influences structure and sets a new context for future behaviour. Archer referred to this as analytical dualism. Although to the casual observer the argument might seem nuanced, the debate about social structure and individual agency continues to this day. Irrespective of one's position, human behaviour cannot be fully explained by social structure or individual agency alone. Against this backdrop, in this book theories of psychology and sociology that intersect with social psychology are presented. In inviting the reader to consider both theory that addresses social structure and individual agency, it is hoped that the researcher will develop a richer meta-theoretical view.

On a cautionary note, it can be difficult to join up the dots from theory that looks at structure and those that address individual agency, where different concepts will be used to explain behaviour. That said, a lack of consistency between theories should not be an impediment to considering different theoretical perspectives; rather, through pragmatism, researchers should seek to view the research problem through multiple and complementary lenses.

1.3 The plan of the book

1.3.1 Aims of the book

Social scientists can be poor communicators, often failing to engage in public discourse about their work in a meaningful way. Theory is symptomatic of this problem, where theory is inward-focused, written by academics for academics, using different language and syntax to expound theory. Moreover, despite a progressive move towards more applied research, theory largely addresses theo-retical problems.

The aim of this book is to address some of the above shortcomings and intro-duce theory in an accessible manner and demonstrate the practical application of theory in real-world settings. Although this is clearly an ambitious aim, it is hoped that the reader will gain an appreciation of the critical role of theory in explaining human behaviour.

As noted, the reader is invited to consider not only psychology but sociol-ogy theory that intersects social psychology. Such an approach will foster more expansive thinking, encourage researchers to consider new avenues of investiga-tion, develop more dynamic and challenging hypotheses to test and ultimately result in more insightful outcomes. There are an innumerable number of theories to explain social structure and individual agency, and it is not possible to include them all within a single source text. Whilst this might seem an obvious flaw, this book is practice-led, where theory that has logical application to market research is presented. Moreover, it is hoped that in reading this book, researchers will be inspired to seek out and explore theory in greater depth.

1.3.2 Book content

In the next chapter, theory that looks at how social influence creates and sus-tains behaviour is considered, where social norms and identity are discussed along with theory that addresses social interactions and habitual behaviour. This is followed by a review of personality theory, where theory is used to explain behavioural tendencies. The focus then turns to theories of motivation, including theories that detail the process of motivation and those that seek to explain the emotions and cognitions that sit behind motivation. In the penul-timate chapter, theory that explains how and why we make judgements about our behaviour and the behaviour of others is examined. In the final chapter, guidance on how to select theory is presented. Although this book is modular in format, it is designed as a coherent whole, where the reader can select specific chapters that are relevant to their field of enquiry or choose to review the book in its entirety.

1.4 References/further reading

Archer, M. S. (1995). *Realist Social Theory: The Morphogenetic Approach*. Cambridge: Cambridge University Press.

Giddens, A. (1984). *The Constitution of Society*. Berkeley: University of California Press.

Kuhn, T. S. (1962; reprint, 2012). *The Structure of Scientific Revolutions*. Chicago, IL: University of Chicago Press.

Chapter 2

How social influence creates and sustains behaviour

CHAPTER OVERVIEW

Key theories: socialisation, social norm theory, pluralistic ignorance, nudge theory, norm following, norm compliance, ethnocentrism, social identity theory, symbolic interactionism, structuration theory and social practice theory.

2.1 We begin by considering the nature of social norms. Different types of norms and norms in different situations are discussed before looking at the power of social norms to change behaviour.

2.2 Next, the role of non-instrumental behaviour and normative influence is discussed.

2.3 We then turn to the role of conformity in avoiding negative consequences of not abiding by social norms.

2.4 Looking next at social identity we explore how we make sense of the social world by dividing the world into 'us' and 'them'.

2.5 In the penultimate chapter, we look at symbolic interactionism and how we ascribe meaning to things based on social interactions.

2.6 Finally, we look at social practice theory as a mechanism in which to understand everyday habitual behaviour.

 DOI: 10.4324/9781003169932-2

Introduction

Social influence is a critical force in human behaviour. To put this in perspective, whenever people interact with one another, they influence each other's attitudes, beliefs and behaviours. To a large extent, the expectations of others influence how we behave. Further, the very act of interacting with others helps give meaning to things and allows us to learn about ourselves and the social world we inhabit.

Why is social influence important in behavioural research?

Upon reading this chapter, the importance of the social context of behaviour will become clear. In market research, there can be a tendency to focus more on the individual and less on the context in which behaviour originated, simply because that is what is most immediately obvious to the researcher when observing behaviour. Gaining an appreciation of societal influences on behaviour is critically important in our understanding of why people do what they do and how they seek to rationalise that behaviour. As we will see, understanding the social context of behaviour can be a powerful tool with which to influence behaviour.

In the beginning

In the 4th century BC, Aristotle compiled a list of social influence techniques in his book, *Rhetoric*. The book was influential in informing the art of persuasion in its day. One of the earliest classifications of social influence is by the itinerant teachers/intellectuals of persuasion (the Sophists) dating back to the 5th century BC. In the 20th century, much of the research into social influence was carried out by sociologists. According to the functionalist sociologist, Talcott Parsons, there are social structures that direct social actions. Within the doctrine of functionalism, this is largely considered to be positive for society, whereby social influence is seen to be important in maintaining social equilibrium. In contrast, those from a Marxist school of thought argued that societal structures promote and subjugate individuals to conform to roles defined by social class systems. Today, the study of social influence is a field of interest to sociologists, psychologists and philosophers. Interestingly, the argument about whether societal influence is a force for good or not continues to this day.

2.1 Social norms: understanding the unwritten rules we live by

2.1.1 Defining social norms

There exist a set of unwritten rules that guide behaviour in social settings. These rules are commonly known as social norms. There is considerable research into social norms, amongst both sociologists and psychologists, adopting different research philosophies and, consequently, different approaches to this field of human behaviour. The result is a rather fragmented approach, with no real consensus regarding the definition and influence of social norms on behaviour. Notwithstanding this, researchers agree on one thing, that social norms are important in influencing behaviour.

In principle, it takes a sufficiently large number of people to subscribe to a particular behaviour, for that behaviour to be considered a social norm. Interestingly, a study by Leeds University would seem to suggest that it does not take that many people to influence behaviour. Researchers asked people to walk randomly along a large hall, with a few being given specific instructions on where to walk. Whilst participants were not allowed to communicate with each other and were told to keep an arm's length apart, those with no instruction instinctively followed those who seemed to know where they were going. This would suggest that humans are prone to a form of herd behaviour, analogous to sparrows murmuring or sheep flocking. Remarkably, it was found that it took just 5% to influence a crowd's direction, without the other 95% realising it (University of Leeds Press Office, 2008).

In market research, we often assume that the decisions participants make are determined by informed and rational choices. Whilst to some extent this is true, decisions are often shaped by the expectations of others. In other words, the extent to which we might think behaviour is a product of free will is probably misplaced. Given this, researchers need to have an appreciation of the extent to which social norms are at play. In turn, this will help researchers to better understand the drivers of behaviour.

2.1.2 Reviewing social norm theory

Social norms are not only unwritten but often illicit behaviour with little conscious thought; as such, social norms might seem somewhat nebulous in nature. If we are to understand social norms, we must start by considering different norm definitions. There are many different norm definitions; indeed, it could be argued that norms have been overdetermined by academics, such that the difference between definitions can seem nuanced. Nonetheless, by considering different norm definitions, we can begin to understand the nature of social norms.

2.1.2.1 Norm definitions

2.1.2.1.1 FORMAL VERSUS INFORMAL NORMS

Academics distinguish between formal and informal norms:

- Formal norms are known, and they are laws that govern society, where not abiding by these laws will result in sanctions.
- Informal norms are likewise known, but not necessarily imposed, although, not abiding by an informal norm can result in judgement, censor even banishment.

The above definitions suggest that social norms are informal norms, where we have a choice about whether to acquiesce or transgress in any given situation, although as we will see later, not abiding by social norms can have negative consequences.

2.1.2.1.2 PRESCRIPTIVE VERSUS PROSCRIPTIVE NORMS

A distinction is drawn between prescriptive and proscriptive norms:

- Prescriptive norms are rules that guide behaviour that is considered societally acceptable (e.g. covering one's mouth when sneezing, giving up your seat to a pregnant person on a train or shaking hands when you meet someone).
- Proscriptive norms are rules that guide behaviour that is considered societally unacceptable (e.g. spitting on the pavement, standing too close to someone you are not acquainted with or eating with your mouth open).

Against the above definition, social norms are both prescriptive and proscriptive in nature. Both norms are culturally dependent. For instance, men holding hands in India is common and is a prescriptive norm, although in America, such behaviour would be frowned upon and thus is a proscriptive norm. Prescriptive and proscriptive norms change over time. For instance, in Victorian times the upper classes would put young boys in dresses until they were 'breeched' at the age of four, where they would be adorned with a set of breeches and a jacket. Notwithstanding more liberal views on gender and identity, we associate wearing a dress more commonly with girls and would be generally uncomfortable with the idea of young boys in dresses.

2.1.2.1.3 DESCRIPTIVE VERSUS INJUNCTIVE NORMS

The Professor Emeritus of Psychology and Marketing at Arizona State University, Robert Cialdini and his colleagues (1990) distinguish between the 'is' (descriptive) and the 'ought' (injunctive) norms.

- Descriptive norms refer to the perception of what is typical, normal, in any given situation. This is based on observing other people's behaviour, including the frequency of behaviour.
- Injunctive norms refer to the rules or beliefs as to what ought to be appropriate behaviour.

Injunctive norms are like prescriptive norms where they deal with behaviour that we approve of and as such, social norms are both descriptive and injunctive in nature.

2.1.2.2 Social norms in different settings

Social norms operate in different social settings. Within a single social sphere, there will be a vast array of social norms based on clearly defined situational factors. Take, for instance, behaviour in public, there is an infinite number of social norms at play, including:

- Apologising if you bump into someone.
- Not talking over people.
- Helping an elderly person cross the road.
- Giving your seat up to a pregnant woman on a bus.
- Not invading people's personal space.
- Exchanging verbal signs, for example, smiling and laughing.
- Shaking hands with someone as a form of greeting.
- Saying 'please' and 'thank you'.

Without exception, there are social norms for all social spheres of human behaviour. For instance, in the occupational environment, we find a set of discrete social norms at play, including:

- Abiding by the company dress code.
- Being professional.
- Arriving on time each day.
- Keeping a positive attitude.
- Respecting senior staff.
- Informing your superior if you are unwell and unable to attend work.
- Avoiding conflict.
- Saying 'hello' and 'goodbye' to colleagues.

2.1.2.3 Learning social norms through socialisation

We learn social norms through socialisation. At its simplest, socialisation is a process where we learn what is acceptable and unacceptable behaviour in the social

Figure 2.1 Agents of socialisation

world. Sociologists talk of agents of socialisation. Agents are specific groups or institutions that help to foster socialisation. The key agents of socialisation are detailed in Figure 2.1.

Both sociologists and developmental psychologists are concerned with how socialisation occurs during childhood and as adults, which is referred to as primary and secondary socialisation, respectively. Primary and secondary socialisation are defined as follows:

■ Primary socialisation: occurs inside the family setting, as a child, we learn from our parents and siblings, and they teach us right from wrong and direct behaviour with the use of rewards and punishments. Naturally, this form of socialisation happens just this once.

■ Secondary socialisation: occurs outside the family setting, we learn from other agents of socialisation. For example, religion promotes moral values regarding behaviour and what is deemed as right and wrong. Education teaches us to appreciate the views of others and the importance of a work ethic. Mass media teaches us about consumption and provides us with role models to aspire to/identify with. This form of socialisation can happen more than once depending on the different social worlds we inhabit.

Culture is an important agent of both primary and secondary socialisation. For example, culture helps set expectations of what constitutes an acceptable emotional response. There are injunctive norms that imply what we 'ought' to feel, towards whom, in what way and for how long. These norms are socially created and defined by culture. Culture provides us with a script that dictates what type, frequency and depth of emotional displays are acceptable in different contexts. For example, different cultures have contrasting expectations regarding grieving for a loved one at a funeral. Some cultures expect a dignified and sombre funeral, whilst others welcome mourners to openly express their grief. Such conventions for emotional expression go largely unnoticed. It is only when a rule is broken, does it come to our attention. This might happen when we enter a new situation where we are not familiar with the expectations or where socialisation has taught us a different emotional response, incongruous with the expected emotional response of the group.

It is important to note that we are not unwitting recipients of cultural influence. We can choose to go with culture, or reject it, although mostly we choose to accept cultural influence. Whether we choose to reject certain cultural practices will be context-dependent. For example, a young Indian woman living in a multicultural society might choose to wear the traditional Indian dress, bindi and bangles at home but when at college, adopt a more western attire, for fear of disparaging remarks from fellow students from different cultures.

2.1.2.4 The role of reference groups and normative influence

Sociologists define a reference group as a group that an individual or another group use as a benchmark in which to compare and contrast their own behaviour. This process of making social comparisons is thought to be important in framing our behaviour and helping us define our sense of self. Within any given reference group, there will be social norms that allude to expectations and behaviour. We have expectations about how we think the reference group behaves and how we think the reference group expects us to behave (as illustrated in Figure 2.2). Typically, a reference group is a group that we look up to and wish to emulate; given this, the expectations of reference groups matter to us.

A peer group is an example of a reference group, that is, a group of people that are similar in terms of age, background, interests and so on. Within this group, we pay attention to the groups' behaviour, which might include, what people wear, what music they listen to, what they do with their spare time which provides us with social cues for determining acceptable behaviour within that

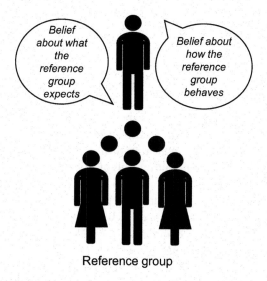

Reference group

Figure 2.2 Reference group expectations

group. Naturally, we will have more than one reference group, including family, college friends, work colleagues, sports teammates, neighbourhoods, celebrities and endorsers, with separate social norms for each.

2.1.2.5 The dynamic nature of social norms

Social norms are dynamic in nature, responding to changes in the environment in which they operate. Take the example of Covid-19, governments the world over instructed us to socially distance to contain the spread of the virus, reduce the stress on health care systems and ultimately reduce the number of deaths from the virus. With such dramatic changes in how we live our lives, it is perhaps unsurprising that new social norms emerge. The most obvious example of this is the replacement of the customary handshake, with an elbow bump, as a form of greeting. In this instance, the reference group included politicians and professional sport's people who publicly adopted elbow bumps.

2.1.2.6 Wesley Perkins and Alan Berkowitz's social norm theory

Social norm theory was first proposed by Perkins and Berkowitz in the mid-1980s to explain alcohol consumption amongst college students in America. The theory is best understood as an approach to harnessing the power of social norms to encourage positive behavioural change (Perkins and Berkowitz, 1986). The theory identifies situational and peer influence as behavioural levers to modifying behaviour. There are two key assumptions to the theory:

- Peer pressure: the influence of others will have a significant impact on behaviour.
- Misconceptions: our perceptions about how others think and act are often out of kilter with reality. For instance, we might overestimate the prevalence of a particular behaviour, which, in turn, results in problematic behaviour, in the case of alcohol, unhealthy levels of drinking.

The theory intimates that by controlling for peer pressure and addressing normative misconceptions, behaviour change can be affected. For example, when there are normative misconceptions, communicating the real social norm helps individuals to express views that are consistent with that social norm and, consequently, reduce the chances of problematic behaviour.

2.1.2.7 Misconceptions and the power of pluralistic ignorance

As suggested by Perkins and Berkowitz (1986), misconceptions of what constitutes normative behaviour can lead to inappropriate behaviour that in turn results in negative consequences. One of the more interesting consequences of misconceptions, is pluralistic ignorance, a phenomenon where members of a group privately reject a social norm but abide by it publicly, erroneously believing that the majority do not share their view. Hans Christian Anderson's fairy tale *The Emperor's New Clothes* is often cited as an example of pluralistic ignorance. Two con artists convince the Emperor that they are the finest clothes makers in all the land. They proceed to acquire gold, silk and other precious items under the ruse of making clothes for the Emperor. When no new clothes are forthcoming, the tailors convince the Emperor that the clothes are invisible to those who are unfit for their positions, stupid, or incompetent. We all know what happens next, the Emperor's subjects, at the risk of looking stupid or unfit, say how beautiful and dazzling the outfit is, knowing full well there is no outfit. It is only when a child points out that the Emperor is wearing no clothes, does the charade come to an end. Clearly, this is a fictional tale; later in this chapter, we look at examples of pluralistic ignorance in the real world.

2.1.2.8 Nudge theory

Nudge theory is cast from the mould of behavioural economics and heuristics, which in turn owes much to cognitive and social psychology. Nudge theory proposes nudges in the form of indirect suggestions and positive reinforcement to influence behaviour. Nudge theory is based on the notion of libertarian paternalism, in which people can be helped to make better decisions by being offered choices that have been designed to enable those choices. The key to nudge theory is the social proof heuristic. According to this heuristic, when people do not know the appropriate way to behave, they defer to others, to provide guidance and direct behaviour. It follows that providing simple normative 'nudges' in terms of what is seen as appropriate behaviour can influence behaviour.

The nudge concept is popularised in Thaler and Sunstein's book *Nudge: Improving Decisions About Health, Wealth, and Happiness* (2008). Nudge theory can be applied to any setting where we are attempting to influence social behaviour. Consequently, the application of nudge theory has been far-reaching. In the 2010s, the United Kingdom's Prime Minister, David Cameron used nudge theory to help administer social policy. Specifically, the United Kingdom's Cabinet Office set up the behavioural insights team, better known as the 'nudge unit'. The aim was to use behavioural economics to persuade people to behave in more socially responsible ways. For instance, to reduce the number of untaxed cars on the roads, the following message was advertised 'Pay your tax or lose your Ford Fiesta'. The message was accompanied by a photo of an untaxed car, the result was a reduction in untaxed cars on the United Kingdom's roads. In another example, those that had failed to pay taxes were sent a letter explaining how their taxes would fund local services, and again, this had the desired effect, by clawing back overdue tax payments to the tune of £200m.

How choices are presented to individuals is referred to as choice architecture. In essence, choice architecture is the design of nudges to elicit the desired choice, and the examples include:

■ Default option: presenting the desired choice as a default; for example, presenting workplace pensions as an opt-out (rather than an opt-in) significantly increases participation.

■ Incentivisation: offering incentives to purchase can act as an effective nudge; for example, supermarkets use in-store advertising to nudge consumers into purchasing products they might not have otherwise considered.

■ Limiting options: it is largely acknowledged that consumer choice is more effective when there are fewer choices to consider, and as such, simply reducing the options will act as a nudge.

■ Marketing: how a product is marketed can act as a nudge. The marketing message can highlight specific features of a product or service. For example, labelling a product as 'low in salt' or 'low in sugar' might appeal to the health-conscious consumer.

Later in this chapter, we look at other examples of nudge theory in action.

There are a few issues to be mindful of when applying nudge theory:

- The premise of helping people make better decisions does raise an intriguing moral question about who should be nudged and in what way.
- Often the desired behavioural changes are temporary unless reinforcement is continuous. As such, adopting nudge like interventions might simply be a quick win but a false economy in the long term.
- The theory oversimplifies behaviour by ignoring the context of behaviour. This has the potential to degrade the impact of the nudge at that moment, or even result in the opposite of the desired effect.
- The theory assumes that the target is a passive recipient of nudges or suggestions. Long-term change requires appealing to hearts and minds.

2.1.3 Measuring social norms in behavioural research

2.1.3.1 Direct observation

Direct observation is one possible approach to measuring social norms. Such an approach can provide rich contextual data that a qualitative interview or group would not be able to offer. The success of direct observation is a product of careful planning and execution. In Figure 2.3, the key steps to direct observation are detailed.

On a cautionary note, the influence of social norms cannot be inferred from observation alone; it would not be unreasonable for someone to behave in a similar fashion to others not because of what the reference groups expect of them, but for some other reason that is not immediately obvious to the researcher. Further, direct observation is not without its problems; not all behaviour is accessible to the researcher and making sense of observed behaviour is difficult even for the most skilled researcher. Nonetheless, direct observation should not be dismissed out of hand, but considered as part of a wider research approach, including qualitative and quantitative measures, as discussed below.

2.1.3.2 Qualitative immersion

Focus groups or one-to-one interviews provide an open and organic environment in which to ask questions and tease out possible nuances in response by a situation; however, asking people about their behaviour comes with its own problems. The reasons why we adhere to social norms is not always immediately obvious. In such instances, we are prone to post-rationalisation, where we 'rationalise'

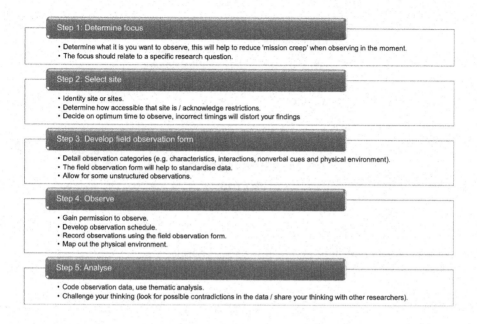

Figure 2.3 Key stages to direct observation

behaviour without knowing why we behaved the way we did in the first place (we will return to the issue of post-rationalisation in Section 4.5). The moderator will need to be cognisant of a possible self-reporting bias (participants might over- or under-report behaviour to be seen to be behaving in a socially desirable manner, ironically, often as a product of normative influence). Alternatively, presenting participants with salient hypothetical scenarios to discuss can help to identify beliefs and social expectations of participants. For instance, a moderator shares different hypothetical scenarios and asks participants to indicate how they think the social actors in the scenario should act.

2.1.3.3 *Quantitative measurement*

Many of the questions asked in a qualitative environment can be formulated into a discrete battery of structured questions and tested in a quantitative survey. Time and budget permitting, using qualitative research to test the structured questions (and response scales) prior to launching the quantitative study, will help to improve the validity and reliability of the measures used.

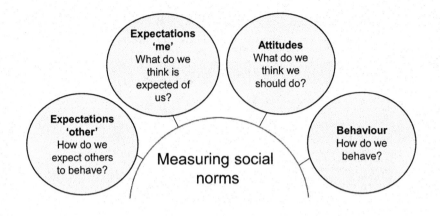

Figure 2.4 Key questions in measuring social norms

Irrespective of the approach, there are broadly four core question areas when looking at social norms, as illustrated in Figure 2.4.

The task of the researcher is to identify what is construed to be the reference group, and then proceed to identify participant's beliefs and assumed social expectations of that reference group.

2.1.4 Social norms theory in action

Below, we look at examples of using social norms as a tool in which to change behaviour. Not only do the examples presented below help illustrate the power of harnessing social norms to modulate behaviour, but they demonstrate just how broad the application of such an approach is. It could be argued that wherever there is a prevailing social norm there is an opportunity to influence behaviour.

2.1.4.1 Harnessing the power of socialisation in the workplace

A multinational company was concerned with how well new employees adjusted to the organisation's culture. It was hypothesised that new employees who adjust quickly would be more productive and committed. Qualitative interviews were conducted amongst new employees along with immediate team members and supervisors. Naturally, when new employees started at the organisation, they were not aware of the social norms existing there. Initially, new employees went through an immersion stage where they learnt the organisational norms. Only then could the new employees begin to accommodate and adapt to the prevailing social norms in the organisation. The study identified a set of social norms that new employees could easily pick up on, which were assumed to be common to most workplace environments:

- Arriving for work in the appropriate dress code.
- Arriving to work on time.
- Being honest and transparent.
- Respecting fellow colleagues.
- Avoiding conflict.
- Greeting colleagues.

Additionally, there were normative influences that were more nuanced, about how staff interacted with senior management, what language was deemed appropriate, what constituted good humour and what was considered inappropriate. These social norms took longer to learn and accommodate.

The study made clear the importance of ensuring that a supportive environment is put in place to help facilitate work socialisation. It was concluded that a smooth socialisation process conferred several advantages, including:

- Helping new employees become accustomed to the culture, values and social norms of the organisation.
- Reducing the chance of conflict between new employees and the organisation.
- Ensuring stability in the organisation.
- Helping to promote working relationships amongst employees.
- Helping to foster employee commitment and productivity.

2.1.4.2 *Addressing teenage pregnancy*

Akella and Jordan (2015) looked at teenage pregnancy and social norms in America. Interviews were conducted amongst pregnant teenagers from economically poor backgrounds, with relatively low educational attainment. The researchers looked at why teenagers became pregnant rather than continue education or secure employment. The outcomes from the interviews suggested that teenage pregnancy was more acceptable when the teenager's mother had also become pregnant at a similar age. Many of the classmates were supportive of the young mums, with some in a similar situation. It was argued by the pregnant teenagers that by becoming pregnant their boyfriends would be more inclined to stay around and support them. The results illustrate the power of parental (mothers of the teenagers) and peer (classmates) role models in reinforcing normative behaviour. Akella and Jordon concluded that more positive role models should be introduced to dissuade teenagers from becoming pregnant.

2.1.4.3 Reducing the incidences of obesity

In response to the worldwide increase in obesity, there has been considerable research into the role of social influence and obesity. Typically, it has been found that weight increase is causally linked to changes in societal values and social norms associated with weight. As the average weight of people has increased, our acceptance of what constitutes a healthy weight has changed correspondingly. It is thought that our acceptance of what constitutes an acceptable weight is influenced by our immediate and wider peer group. Maximova et al. (2008) observed that higher BMI scores for parents and friends correlated with a greater misconception of weight status amongst both children and adolescents. In other words, children and adolescents were less likely to consider themselves obese if they were surrounded by obese people. This study and others similar to it highlight the importance of challenging established social norms associated with weight.

Below are examples of using nudges and positive reinforcement to influence behaviour.

2.1.4.4 Reducing men's urinal spillages

The use of fly shapes in the men's urinals at Amsterdam's Schiphol airport to reduce spillages is synonymous with nudge theory. The premise was simple; if men are presented with a target, they will aim for it, and in so doing, spillages would be reduced. Small fly shapes were etched into the porcelain of the men's urinals, near the drain. This relatively simple nudge reduced spillages by up to 80%. A manager at the airport recommended the idea to the airport's board of directors and attributed the idea to a Dutch maintenance person, who had served in the Dutch army in the 1960s and had observed the use of small red dots in the urinals to reduce 'misdirection'.

2.1.4.5 Reducing patient no-shows

Patients not turning up to appointments is a significant problem for the United Kingdom's National Health Service (NHS). Around six million people fail to honour their appointment every year. It is estimated that this costs the NHS £700 million a year. Patient surveys looking into this problem suggest that whilst some patients get better and others struggle with the process or have feelings of anxiety, most simply forget to turn up. To address this, a trial was conducted amongst doctor's surgeries in the NHS Bedfordshire trust, where different types of nudges were tested (Martin et al., 2012). The receptionists in the doctor's surgeries were instructed to change the language used when booking appointments, so the patient felt more involved in the process. Additionally, patients were encouraged to complete their own appointment cards. These behavioural interventions helped to reduce the no show rate. Interestingly, it was common practice amongst surgeries to publicise the level of no-shows per month either on the walls or on a TV in the waiting rooms, to shame people into action by appealing to their sense of responsibility. However, this served to normalise the behaviour. To counter this, posters detailing how many people had turned up for their appointment in previous months were trialled in the surgeries. This intervention was found to be more effective than any other, resulting in a significant fall in no-shows.

2.1.4.6 Encouraging paying tax on time

In the United Kingdom, Her Majesty's Revenue and Customs (HMRC) had a problem, many people were not paying their tax bills on time. Sending numerous reminders/threats had limited effect. To address this problem, those with arrears were sent messages along the lines of '9 out of 10 people pay their tax on time' (Cabinet Office, Behavioural Insight Team, 2012). The rationale was that those that were in arrears would feel uncomfortable because they were not abiding by the social norm, where most people pay their taxes on time, the assumption being that instinctively people want to comply to a social norm and would consequently 'pay up'. Encouragingly, the messaging resulted in a 15% increase in tax payments.

2.1.4.7 Virgin Atlantic aviation fuel reduction field study

In 2014, the carrier Virgin Atlantic worked with economists from the University of Chicago and the London School of Economics to help reduce jet fuel consumption (Gosnell et al., 2016). The amount of fuel used is to some extent a product of how the pilot chooses to fly the plane, for example, changing altitude or turning off some of the engines when taxiing at the airport helps to reduce fuel consumption. A field study was set up involving 335 pilots. The pilots were randomly assigned to various nudge conditions. Some pilots were sent monthly reports of fuel consumption to their home addresses, whilst others received personalised targets and were able to make charity donations if they met those targets. Additionally, a control group received no nudging. The pilot's fuel consumption was measured prior to the beginning of the trial (to provide the researchers with a consumption benchmark), during the trial and six months after the trial. The study resulted in a drop in fuel consumption and a reduction of carbon dioxide emissions of 21,500 tons. Even after the study was completed, fuel consumption savings continued to be made. Logic would dictate that fuel consumption amongst those in the control group would not have changed markedly; however, like those that were 'nudged', fuel consumption improved. The authors suggested that this was a result of the Hawthorne effect (a phenomenon where participants behave differently in response to knowing they are part of the study), where 'being monitored' was sufficient to reduce fuel consumption. Thus, it would seem the very act of being monitored worked as a nudge.

Next, we look at some examples of pluralistic ignorance.

2.1.4.8 Addressing climate change

We have known about the impact of climate change for the best part of 50 years, yet our response to climate change does not reflect the gravity of the situation indicated by science. One possible explanation is pluralistic ignorance. Until recently, the majority have remained largely silent, with many who had genuine concerns about climate change believing that their views were (incorrectly) in the minority. It is thought that silence by the majority is to ensure that the individual is not perceived as less competent when discussing issues about climate change. In turn, pluralistic ignorance inhibits engagement in collective actions.

2.1.4.9 Reducing alcohol consumption in college

Another example of pluralistic ignorance is college student's drinking habits. Alcohol use is common at most colleges and universities in the United Kingdom, but exactly how common is it? The National Union of Students conducted a study into students' relationship with alcohol (NUS Alcohol Impact: Students and Alcohol Survey, 2018). They found that although alcohol use was common, many reported not consuming alcohol at all. It was also observed that there was an expectation that students get drunk and that this behaviour is an implicit part of student culture. Peer pressure was a factor. Over three-quarters of the students interviewed stated they drank alcohol to fit in with their peers. The high visibility of the university drinking culture and a reluctance of students to show any public expression of disapproval can lead to pluralistic ignorance. In reality, college students overestimate the frequency and quantity of consumption along with the extent of approval of such drinking. In so doing, students help to perpetuate the prevailing social norm, erroneously believing that all college students support heavy drinking. Interestingly, communicating the actual statistics for student alcohol consumption helps dispel the myth and counter pluralistic ignorance.

2.1.5 Implications for behavioural research

1   In market research, there can be a tendency to focus more on the individual and less on the social context from which behaviour originated, simply because that is what is most immediately obvious to the researcher when observing behaviour.

2   Key to social influence are social norms. Social norms make clear what is acceptable and what is not, by different reference groups. If researchers are to understand behaviour, they must seek to understand the role of reference groups in directing behaviour.

3   The various examples detailed in this chapter demonstrate how social norms can be used to encourage positive behavioural change in different settings.

4   Participant observation can be effective in observing normative behaviour, although consideration should be given to augmenting this with qualitative or quantitative research.

5   Asking participants to explain why they behave in a particular way might result in little more than truism and conjecture. Presenting participants with salient hypothetical scenarios can help to unearth a participant's understanding of what is expected of them in different social contexts.

2.1.6 References/further reading

Akella, D., and Jordan, M. (2015). Impact of Social and Cultural Factors on Teenage Pregnancy. *Journal of Health Disparities Research and Practice*, 8 (1), pp. 41–62.

Cabinet Office: Behavioural Insights Team. (2012). *Applying Behavioural Insights to Reduce Fraud, Error and Debt*. https://www.gov.uk/government/publications/fraud-error-and-debt-behavioural-insights-team-paper [accessed 1/05/2020].

Cialdini, R. B., Kallgren, C, A., and Reno, R. R. (1990). A Focus Theory of Normative Conduct: A Theoretical Refinement and Reevaluation of the Role of Norms in Human Behavior. *Advances in Experimental Social Psychology*, 24, pp. 201–234.

Gosnell, G. K., List, J. A., and Metcalfe, R. (2016). *A New Approach to an Age-Old Problem: Solving Externalities by Incenting Workers Directly.* National Bureau of Economic Research, Working Paper 22316.

Martin, S., Bassi, S., and Dunbar-Rees, R. (2012). Commitments, Norms and Custard Creams – A Social Influence Approach to Reducing Did Not Attends (DNAs). *Journal of the Royal Society of Medicine*, 105 (3), pp. 101–104.

Maximova, K., McGrath, J. J., Barnett, O'Loughlin T., Paradis, J. G., and Lambert, M. (2008). Do You See What I See? Weight Status Misperception and Exposure to Obesity Among Children and Adolescents. *International Journal of Obesity*, 32 (6), pp. 1008–1015.

Perkins, H. W., and Berkowitz, A. D. (1986). Perceiving the Community Norms of Alcohol Use among Students: Some Research Implications for Campus Alcohol Education Programming. *International Journal of Addiction*, 21 (9–10), pp. 961–976.

Thaler, R., and Sunstein, C. (2008). *Nudge: Improving Decisions About Health, Wealth, and Happiness*. London: Penguin House.

University of Leeds Press Office. (2008). Sheep in Human Clothing – Scientists Reveal Our Flock Mentality. *Society and Politics News*, 14th February. https://www.leeds.ac.uk/news/article/397/sheep_in_human_clothing__scientists_reveal_our_flock_mentality [accessed 21/12/2020].

NUS. (2018). *Alcohol Impact: Students and Alcohol – National Survey*. https://www.nus-connect.org.uk/resources/students-alcohol-national-survey [accessed 6/10/2020].

2.1.6.1 Want to know more?

Reflecting the sheer scale of knowledge in this field there are many good texts on social norms; below are detailed two books that provide a good underpinning to social norms and their importance in social behaviour:

Bicchieri, C. (2016). *Norms in the Wild: How to Diagnose, Measure and Change Social Norms*. Oxford: Oxford University Press.

Cialdini, R. B. (2007). *Influence: The Psychology of Persuasion*. New York: HarperCollins.

2.2 Norm following: defining non-instrumental behaviour

2.2.1 Defining norm following

So far, we have discussed the power of social norms to direct and give meaning to social behaviour. Next, we look at the different ways in which we acquiesce to normative expectations. We could be forgiven for assuming that adhering to a social norm is largely a product of conformity. However, it is important to distinguish between following and conforming to social norms (Brennan et al., 2016). This distinction is made in Figure 2.5.

2.2.2 Reviewing norm following theory

Norm following is a form of non-instrumental behaviour, that is, we adhere to a social norm with no obvious personal loss or benefit, but simply because of the social norm. In this case, the social pressure of others and the possible

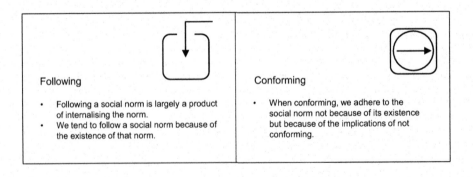

Figure 2.5 Following and conforming to normative influences

consequences of non-conformity has no part in driving behaviour. Irrespective of the nature of the social norm, following is largely an unconscious act, with little or no deliberation. As such, the social norm becomes indistinguishable from our wider personal values and beliefs. Following involves us subscribing to a social norm both publicly and privately and results in behaviour that is deep-seated and permanent.

Following social norms often relates to matters of fairness and reciprocity. For example, when someone does us a favour, we feel compelled to return that favour. This quid pro quo is something we learn during socialisation and is generally considered to be a deep-seated belief that means that we feel duty-bound to reciprocate. Reciprocation is seen as an important rule that helps to sustain order and ensure a sense of fairness in the social world. We feel we have a moral obligation to reciprocate. Intriguingly, reciprocity can even work in instances where the initial favour is unsolicited or from someone we do not even like. So strong is the tendency to reciprocate, that it can be used to manipulate behaviour.

2.2.3 *Measuring following in behavioural research*

2.2.3.1 *Economic games*

Reciprocity and fairness have been measured by experimental economists who use economic games, such as the ultimatum and the dictator game, to test whether behaviour is a product of self-interest or bound by reciprocity and fairness. The outcomes from these games make clear that human behaviour significantly deviates from economic models of self-interest. In the ultimatum game, two people are randomly assigned the role of proposer and receiver, the proposer is given an amount of money and must choose an amount to share with the receiver. If the receiver agrees to the amount, then they both get to keep the money. If the receiver rejects the proposer's offer, then neither keep the money. Mostly, 40–50% is proposed and subsequently accepted, whereby a fair split is the favoured strategy. This experiment and others like it clearly demonstrate non-instrumental behaviour.

2.2.3.2 *Hypothetical scenarios*

Although the outcomes of economic games tell us something of the nature of fairness, they lack ecological validity. In other words, we cannot with confidence, extrapolate the findings from economic games to real-world settings. To understand norm following it will be important to understand the wider personal values and beliefs that define following behaviour. As noted earlier in this chapter, presenting participants with salient hypothetical scenarios to discuss and asking them to indicate how they think the social actors in the scenarios should act, works well to elicit values and beliefs.

2.2.4 Norm following theory in action

2.2.4.1 The Bennington studies

Norm following is important in changing political views. It is notoriously difficult to change people's political views. During election time, political parties invest significant sums of money in media campaigns that try to do just that, often with limited success. It makes more sense to attempt to influence the undecided middle of any political divide, where you are not challenging deeply held views, but persuading people to move a little to the left or the right.

Theodore Newcomb investigated the changing political views of young students at Bennington College, a women's college in Vermont, America. The students were interviewed on multiple occasions between 1935 and 1939 (Newcomb, 1943). Newcomb measured students' attitudes toward social and economic issues over this period. Mostly, the students were from affluent middle-class backgrounds with over two-thirds of the students' parents affiliated with the Republican party. The students encountered older students and faculty members who held liberal, social, economic and political views. Over time, the students' political position moved progressively to the left of their parents.

The older students and faculty members acted as the reference group, which set expectations of behaviour. Initially, the students chose to go along with the social norm to fit in, rather than because of a fundamentally deep-seated change of political ideology. However, over time, the students moved from conformity to following as they began to internalise the values and beliefs of their new peer group.

There were follow-up studies with Bennington alumni, at 25- and 50-year intervals (Duane et al., 2006). The results from these studies suggested that the change in political ideology was stable. Moreover, many of the alumni had married partners who shared their liberal political views, thus providing a new reference group to further support those views.

2.2.4.2 Norm following and marketing

Fairness and reciprocity are used as a mechanism in which to encourage product purchase, as illustrated in Table 2.1.

Fairness and reciprocation are important tools for marketeers, and shows that effective marketing is about value exchange.

2.2.5 Implications for behavioural research

1 Following social norms is a form of non-instrumental behaviour. That is, we follow a social norm, not because of the consequences of not adhering to it but because of the social norm. In this instance, the social norm is indistinguishable from our wider values and beliefs.

Table 2.1 Fairness and reciprocity in marketing

Type	Definition
Free sample	• A common marketing technique is to offer a free sample of a product, allowing the consumer to try out and see if they like it. • The consumer is at liberty to decide whether to purchase the product or not. Yet, the free sample was a gift, the power of reciprocation means that we often feel a sense of indebtedness resulting in us purchasing the product, even if we did not like the sample in the first place. • At its simplest, this might be a marketing tweet to engage consumers. If a company tweets a consumer, they will feel inclined to tweet back.
Free trial	• The free trial is a well-established technique. Typically, a consumer tries out a product over a specified time period and if they are not happy with it, they can send it back. • Take, for instance, a free mattress trial for three months; by the end of the free period, a consumer might feel they have gained from being able to use the mattress for three months and consequently, feel obliged to keep the mattress.
Free goody pack	• A common technique for charity fund-raising is to send out a 'free goody pack' which might include, a pen, a fluffy toy or a calendar. • In receiving the goody pack, we appreciate the time and expense that went into it and feel obliged to return the favour in the form of a donation.

2 Although the reasons for social norm following are likely to be deep-seated, relatively simple marketing techniques can be used to appeal to our innate sense of fairness and reciprocity.

3 The outcomes from the Beddington studies suggest that with a strong reference group we can influence behaviour over time, whereby understanding reference groups will help researchers understand how to modulate behaviour.

2.2.6 References/further reading

Brennan, G., Eriksson, L., Goodwin, E., and Southwood, N. (2016). *Explaining Norms*. Oxford: Oxford University Press.

Duane, F. A., Cohen, L. C., and Newcomb, T. M. (2006). *Political Attitudes over the Life Span: The Bennington Women after Fifty Years*. Madison: University of Wisconsin Press.

Newcomb, T. (1943). *Personality and Social Change: Attitude Formation in a Student Community*. New York: Dryden.

2.3 Norm conforming: avoiding censure or punishment

2.3.1 Defining norm conforming

Whilst following a social norm involves non-instrumental behaviour, conforming is mostly about avoiding possible negative consequences of not abiding by a social norm, without the deep-seated agreement associated with following a social norm. In such instances, we go with the flow and accept the prevailing social norm, rather than resist it. Not abiding by a social norm might lead to censure or even punishment.

2.3.2 Reviewing norm conforming theory

With the above definition in mind, there are three different types of conformity.

2.3.2.1 Compliance

An individual accepts the influence of others with an expressed desire to gain a favourable outcome, including avoiding censure or punishment. We might publicly change our behaviour but privately hold a conflicting view; consequently, this is the weakest form of conformity.

2.3.2.2 Identification

Identification is where an individual conforms to the expectations of a social role or archetype, for example, nurse, police officer and teacher. We conform to the assumed expectations of known social roles, which helps to ensure meaningful relationships within a group. Typically, an individual behaves in such a way as to conform to stereotypes depicted in the media. As with compliance, conformity occurs even if the beliefs/values of the group are contrary to that of the individual.

2.3.2.3 Ingratiation

Ingratiation is where we conform to impress or gain favour or acceptance from other people. Rather than acting to avoid punishment, ingratiation is about social manipulation/coercing others to achieve something.

2.3.2.3.1 EDWARD E JONES' THREE-FACTOR MODEL

The social psychologist Jones was concerned with the nature of ingratiation. In his book *Ingratiation: A Social Psychological Analysis* (1964), Jones argued that

Table 2.2 Three factors of ingratiation

Factor	Definition
Self-representation	• We present ourselves in a manner that is thought to be attractive to the recipient. • For example, 'dressing up' or 'going casual' depending on the recipient's assumed tastes.
Opinion-conformity	• Expressing the beliefs and values, or behaviours consistent with others. • This is an indirect form of flattery. • For example, criticising a work colleague that is generally not favoured by the recipient.
Other-enhancement	• Expressing favourable opinions about the recipient. • This is a direct form of flattery. • For example, remembering an individual's name, demonstrating admiration or respect, making clear that you share their opinions, greeting them positively, and maintaining eye contact during a conversation.

the study of ingratiation was important in understanding social interactions and group cohesiveness. He proposed a three-factor model of ingratiation, as illustrated in Table 2.2.

2.3.2.4 Emotions as 'compliance enforcers'

Earlier in this chapter, we discussed the relationship between social norms and emotions where injunctive norms dictate how we 'ought' to feel in different social contexts. Emotions also play a part in reinforcing social norms. When we disapprove of someone's behaviour, we will express this with feelings of disgust, indignation or contempt; the recipient will feel guilt, shame or embarrassment. For compliant behaviour, we seek to praise or express feelings of admiration or gratitude. As such, emotions are key to the maintenance of normative behaviour both in terms of those that are being judged and the recipient.

2.3.2.5 Cultural differences

Perhaps unsurprisingly, there are significant differences in conformity by culture. As a rule of thumb, western societies are less conformist than eastern societies. The reason for this might be that western societies are typically individualistic, whilst eastern societies are more collective. Individualistic societies place a greater emphasis on individual goals and achievement, where strength, self-reliance and assertiveness are valued qualities. In contrast, collectivist societies focus on collective goals, where self-sacrifice, dependability and helping others are valued qualities.

2.3.3 Measuring conformity in behavioural research

Mehrabian and Stefl (1995) have developed a generalised question battery for conformity, comprised of 11 items with an agreement ranging from very strongly agree to very strongly disagree.

2.3.4 Norm conforming theory in action

In the following, we look at some of the classic studies in this field of research, along with some more recent examples.

2.3.4.1 Compliance: Solomon Asch's line experiment

Asch (1951) was concerned with how the influence of others in a social setting would direct behaviour. Asch set up a bogus line judgement task. The task entailed looking at a target line and deciding which of the three comparison lines best matched the target line. Unbeknownst to the subject, the other participants had been instructed to give the same, 'primed' wrong answer. Importantly, each time, the subject sat at the end of the row of participants and gave their answer last. In the control condition, there were no primed participants. There were 18 trials in total and the primed participants gave the wrong answer on 12 trials. A third of the subjects went along with the group whose response was clearly wrong (in the control condition it was only 1%). Many stated that they knew the answer was wrong but feared being ridiculed and assumed the wider group knew more than they did. Consequently, this form of compliance is sometimes known as information conformity. Asch's experiment suggests that social influence can result in people ignoring the most obvious truths to comply.

It has been suggested that the outcomes of Asch's experiment reflected American values of the day in 1950s America defined by McCarthyism. The outcomes of more recent studies replicating Asch's experiment are less conclusive. For example, Perrin and Spencer (1980) replicated the original experiment with engineering, mathematics and chemistry students and found that only in one trial (out of a total of 396 trials) did the participant erroneously go with the majority view. Perrin and Spencer argued that this was owing to a cultural shift in students' beliefs about conformity and obedience. However, the results of Perrin and Spencer's work might say more about the participants of the experiment than a cultural shift, where it is highly likely that students of engineering, mathematics and chemistry would adopt a more 'literal' view of the trial and be less inclined to acquiesce to group pressure. Lalancette and Standing (1990) modified the original experiment to make the task more ambiguous, to increase likelihood of conformity. As in the case of Perrin and Spencer, no conformity was observed. Lalancette and Standing concluded that the Asch effect was an unpredictable phenomenon. In another experiment, Neto (1995) was interested in whether the conformity seen in Asch's experiment would occur in other cultures and not just in America. Again, Asch's experiment was replicated, this time amongst psychology students at a Portuguese university. Over half of the students (59%) conformed at least once in the experimental condition, which was far greater than that observed in the control condition.

2.3.4.2 Compliance and song choice

An obvious flaw of Asch's experiment is a lack of ecological validity. A study by the sociologist Salganik (2006) addresses this issue. The researchers were concerned with why certain songs, books and movies are so much more successful than the average. It would be logical to assume that these products were in some way better than the rest. Intriguingly, experts often fail to identify which songs, books and movies will be successful. The researchers asked 14,341 participants to download previously unknown songs by unknown bands. The experimental group saw previous participants' download choices, the control group did not. Participants were asked to rate the songs using a five-star scale, ranging from one star for 'I hate it' to five stars for 'I love it'. Whilst the best songs rarely did badly and the worst songs rarely did well, quality only partially explained the result, whereby those in the experimental group gave higher ranking for songs that were seen as popular with previous participants. There was no such effect with the control group. In other words, social influence had impacted on the experimental group's responses.

2.3.4.3 Compliance and sequential requests

In marketing, the use of sequential requests is a common tool to engender compliance. There are various techniques used but essentially compliance is achieved by the use of two or more requests. Let us look now at the more common sequential request techniques.

2.3.4.3.1 FOOT-IN-THE-DOOR TECHNIQUE

This is a technique where an initial small request is followed by a larger request. Agreeing to a small request significantly increases the likelihood of agreeing to a larger request further down the line. Take, for instance, if we agree to lend a small amount of money to a friend, we are much more likely to agree to an additional larger request later. The initial request creates a bond between the requester and the requestee, which helps to support the second request. The bond means we feel duty-bound to honour the larger request, even if the decision does not feel rational at the time. This is a technique that is commonplace amongst charities, where people are initially asked to donate a small amount each month and then later, are asked to increase that amount. The implications for marketeers are clear, adopt a marketing strategy that initially asks for very little from the consumer, then slowly build a relationship with a view to driving product purchase.

2.3.4.3.2 DOOR-IN-THE-FACE TECHNIQUE

This technique is a reversed engineered foot-in-the-door technique. Initially, a significant request is made, where it is expected to be rejected. This is followed by a smaller request, which the requestee finds difficult to reject having rejected the first request. In coming up with a smaller request the requester is seen to compromise. It is thought that in rejecting the large request the requestee feels they 'owe' the requester. This technique was tested by Cialdini et al. (1975) where subjects were asked whether they would mentor young offenders for two hours per week for two years, most refused. Another group were asked to escort children around a zoo, again most refused. Another group were asked to mentor young offenders; most refused but shortly after were asked to escort children around a zoo, half agreed to that request.

2.3.4.3.3 LOW-BALLING TECHNIQUE

This is a technique where we are initially presented with an attractive offer, but that offer is subsequently withdrawn and an inferior offer is put in its place. Having committed to the initial offer, we feel compelled to extend our compliance to the less favourable offer. The most cited example is a car salesperson, where the salesperson offers a car at an initially attractive price, but following discussions with the dealership manager, that offer is withdrawn and a less attractive offer is put to the customer.

2.3.4.3.4 THAT'S-NOT-ALL TECHNIQUE

This is a technique where a product is promoted, with an additional offer near the end of the advert to make the offer look better and persuade people to purchase. For instance, if we take a vacuum cleaner advert, the product might be advertised with the addition of free attachments at the end of the advert, to persuade those that were sitting on the fence.

2.3.4.4 *Identification: Philip Zimbardo's Stanford Prison experiment*

Zimbardo was interested in finding out whether the brutality reported among prison guards in America was a product of the guard's personality or more to do with the prison setting (Haney et al., 1973). In 1971, the basement of the psychology department of Stanford University was converted into a prison. Recruits were randomly assigned to one of two groups, prisoner, or guard. All were of sound mind and exhibited no obvious tendencies towards antisocial behaviour. To ensure the experience was authentic, prisoners were arrested in their homes, taken to the prison, stripped naked, deloused and given a prison uniform. They were assigned a prison number and were only referred by this for the duration of the experiment. The prison guards were given uniforms, a whistle and dark sunglasses, and this rendered eye contact between guard and prisoner impossible. The guards were instructed to do what was necessary to maintain order in the prison.

Within a very short period, the guards began to harass the prisoners. On the first night, at 2:30 am prisoners were awakened by the sound of whistles for the first of many prisoner counts. Against a backdrop of increasing harassment and intimidation, prisoners adopted 'prison like behaviour', acquiescing to the prison rules, with some reporting on those that did not obey the rules. By day two, there was outright rebellion, prisoners used their beds to barricade themselves in their cells. The guards forced their way in, stripped the prisoners and removed their beds. Over time, the prisoners became more dependent and the guards were increasingly hostile to the prisoners. One of the prisoners became emotionally unstable, exhibiting disorganised thinking, shaking, uncontrollable crying and rage and was consequently removed from the experiment. Although meant to last two weeks, after just six days, time was called on the experiment. Whilst there are many ethical issues with this experiment, it does make clear just how quickly we conform to stereotypical roles portrayed in the media of the time. As noted, the guards wore darkened sunglasses, ensuring there was no eye contact between guard and prisoner, and this helped to create the illusion of anonymity. The guards felt they could act with impunity, with their actions not discernible from the wider guard group, a phenomenon referred to as de-individualisation.

2.3.4.5 *British Broadcasting Centre (BBC) 2002 Stanford Prison Experiment replication*

The outcomes of Zimbardo's original experiment might reflect the prevailing values and attitudes of the day. To see how people would respond now, Zimbardo's experiment was replicated by the BBC in 2002. The experiment was conducted by the social psychologists Steve Reicher and Alex Haslam. A prison was constructed at Elstree Studios in Hertfordshire, England. This time, care was taken to ensure that no harm came to the participants. An independent committee was set up to oversee the study with the remit to remove participants or call time on the experiment if it was felt that participants were being put under undue stress or in harm's way.

Unlike the original study, there was initially little evidence of prison guards conforming to stereotypical roles. Yet, prisoners exhibited explicit resistance to the guards' regime, culminating in a prison breakout on day six. Upon which, a self-governing commune was set up, this later failed because of internal conflict. Following this, a group of former prisoners and guards wanted to introduce a new harsh authoritarian regime not dissimilar to that seen in the original experiment. It was at this point that it is was decided to call time on the experiment, to safeguard the participants.

The authors concluded that we do not blithely conform to roles; rather, we adopt a role as a product of social identification within a group (Reicher and Haslam, 2006). It is human nature to try and leave the prisoner group. Only when this is not possible, do we start to identify with a group to affect change. The extent to which participants identified with the guard role, is contingent on the accountability for their actions. If there is a chance of disapproval or punishment, either within the context of the experiment or from those in everyday life, then the chances of participants identifying with the stereotypical 'harsh guard' position are reduced.

2.3.4.6 Ingratiation: Hair salon and restaurant tipping

Although flattery can be construed as disingenuous, it is an effective technique even when the recipient is aware that they are being manipulated. Seiter and Dutson (2007) looked at flattery and tipping in a hair salon. In the study, one customer cohort was complimented by the hairdresser, whilst the other was not. The first cohort tended to leave a larger tip, thus demonstrating the power of praise. This outcome has been found in other settings; for example, when waiting staff complemented the restaurant guest's choice of food, a larger tip was often forthcoming (Seiter, 2007).

2.3.5 Implications for behavioural research

1   Conformity is common human behaviour. We conform to avoid censure or punishment. The examples of using conformity as a tool to drive purchase behaviour suggest that relatively simple techniques such as sequential requests and free trials can be effective marketing tools.

2   On a cautionary note, whilst various techniques can be used to influence behaviour, they are unlikely to result in long-term behavioural change. To achieve this, individuals will need to follow social norms.

3   The study into song choice demonstrates how social influence impacts on our choices regarding cultural objects.

4   Traditionally, marketeers have considered conformity regarding the physical world. The advent of social influencers highlights the importance of considering conformity in the online social world.

2.3.6 References/further reading

Asch, S. E. (1951). Effects of Group Pressure upon the Modification and Distortion of Judgments. In H. Guetzkow (Ed.), *Groups, Leadership and Men*, pp. 177–190. Pittsburg, PA: Carnegie Press.

Cialdini, R. B., Vincent, J. E., Lewis, S. K., Catalan, J., Wheeler, D., and Darby, B. L. (1975). Reciprocal Concessions Procedure for Inducing Compliance: The Door-in-the-face Technique. *Journal of Personality and Social Psychology*, 31 (2), pp. 206–215.

Haney, C., Banks, W. C., and Zimbardo, P. G. (1973). A Study of Prisoners and Guards in a Simulated Prison. *Naval Research Review*, 30, pp. 4–17.

Jones, E. E. (1964). *Ingratiation, A Social Psychological Analysis*. New York: Appleton Century Crofts.

Lalancette, M.-F., and Standing, L. (1990). Asch Fails Again. *Social Behavior and Personality: An International Journal*, 18 (1), pp. 7–12.

Mehrabian, A., and Stefl, C. A. (1995). Basic Temperament Components of Loneliness, Shyness, and Conformity. *Social Behavior and Personality: An International Journal*, 23 (3), pp. 253–264.

Neto, F. (1995). Conformity and Independence Revisited. *Social Behavior and Personality*, 23 (3), pp. 217–222.

Perrin, S., and Spencer, C. (1980). The Asch Effect – A Child of Its Time. *Bulletin of the BPS*, 33, pp. 405–406.

Reicher, S., and Haslam, S. A. (2006). Rethinking the Psychology of Tyranny: The BBC Prison Study. *British Journal of Social Psychology*, 45, pp. 1–40.

Salganik, M., Dodds, P., and Watts, D. (2006). Experimental Study of Inequality and Unpredictability in an Artificial Cultural Market. *Science*, 311 (5762), pp. 854–856.

Seiter, S. J. (2007). Ingratiation and Gratuity: The Effect of Complimenting Customers on Tipping Behavior in Restaurants. *Journal of Applied Social Psychology*, 37 (3), pp. 478–485.

Seiter, S. J., and Dutson, E. (2007). The Effect of Compliments on Tipping Behavior in Hairstyling Salons. *Journal of Applied Social Psychology*, 37 (9), pp. 1999–2007.

2.4 Social identity: dividing the world into 'us' and 'them'

2.4.1 Defining social identity

Social identity refers to our sense of self based on perceived membership of social groups. Belonging to different groups helps shape how we see ourselves and others in the social world and is important in supporting self-worth and esteem. We belong to numerous groups including family, political party, football club, occupation, nationality, ethnicity and so on. Intriguingly, it seems we are quick to identify with a group and the process starts from an early age. In this chapter, we look at ethnocentrism and social identity theory before reviewing examples of social identity in action.

2.4.2 Reviewing social identity theory

2.4.2.1 William Sumner's in-groups, out-groups and ethnocentrism

Sumner first alluded to in-groups and out-groups in his book *Folkways: A Study of the Sociological Importance of Usages, Manners, Customs, Mores, and Morals* (1906). In-groups are social groups that we feel we belong to and out-groups are social groups we do not feel we belong to. Whatever group we belong to, there are social norms that define what is acceptable behaviour in that group; in adhering to the social norms of the group, we implicitly identify with that group. There is a tendency to view the out-group through the lens of the in-group. This is at least partly based on the assumption that the social norms and values of the in-group are valid and universal. Further, we tend to assume that the social norms and values of the in-group are superior to the out-group. Sumner called this ethnocentrism.

Ethnocentrism helps to create in-group cohesion and continuity, although it can lead to misunderstanding, feelings of distain and even the adoption of prejudicial views towards the out-group. British colonialism is often cited as an example of ethnocentrism, where the British considered the indigenous populations of the colonies as backward, in need of western enlightenment and technological innovation. For example, a view of Indian culture through the narrow lens of the Victorian intellectual classes meant that the British failed to appreciate Hindu customs and culture, with many Victorians referring to them as barbaric and unchristian. To 'replicate' in-group values and practices, many rules and regulations from Britain were imported, including the penal code banning homosexuality, that prior to British colonisation, was generally accepted in Indian culture.

2.4.2.2 Henri Tajfel's social identity theory

The phenomenon of ethnocentrism has been hugely influential in social psychology, where theories to explain intergroup relations, prejudice and conflict have been developed, including social identity theory. Like Sumner, the social psychologist Tajfel proposed that to support our sense of self-worth and esteem, we promote the groups we belong to and adopt prejudicial views of those that we do not belong to. This is a process of dividing the social world into 'us' and 'them'. Examples of this include:

- Football club: Celtic versus Rangers.
- Political party: Republicans versus Democrats.
- Religion: Catholics versus Protestants.
- Tribe: Hutus versus Tutsis.
- Country: Bosnians versus Serbs.
- Social class: middle versus working class.

Social identity theory evolved from a series of minimal-group studies conducted by Tajfel and his colleagues in the early 1970s. The minimal-group method is designed to identify the minimal conditions required for in-group bias to occur. Typically, participants are randomly assigned to one of two groups based on relatively arbitrary categories, for example, colour preference or the toss of a coin. As such, participants are assigned to novel groups where there is nothing to fundamentally distinguish one group from another. Further, members of each group remain anonymous, with no social interaction prior to or during the experiment. Notwithstanding this, participants exhibited in-group favouritism and out-group prejudice, for example, when asked to allocate resources, such as money or points, participants allocated more resources to the in-group than the out-group. Intriguingly, the simple act of being categorised, on relatively meaningless grounds, is sufficient to create in-group bias.

Tajfel and Turner suggested there are three mental processes that we go through to establish an 'us' and 'them' view (Tajfel and Turner, 1979). Each stage is presented in Figure 2.6.

There is also a phenomenon where likeable members of the in-group are viewed more favourably and deviant members less favourably, when compared to similar out-group members. In other words, judgements about in-group members are more extreme than judgements about out-group members. It is thought that this helps to protect the identity of the in-group.

2.4.2.3 Irving Janis' groupthink

It was in Janis' 1972 book *Victims of Groupthink*, the phrase 'groupthink' was first coined (in reference to 'doublethink' from George Orwell's dystopian novel, *1984*). The phrase refers to an excessive form of concurrence-seeking amongst group members, to such an extent that the views, opinions and beliefs outside the group are largely ignored. Janis attributed a number of American foreign policy decisions, including the Imperial Japanese Navy attack on Pearl Harbour (1941),

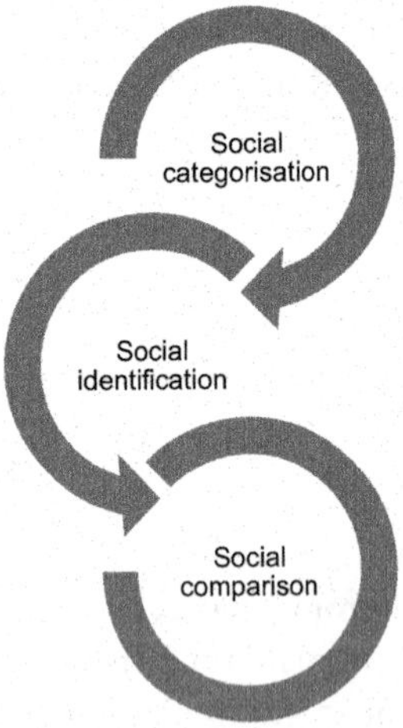

Social categorisation
- To conform to the social norms of a group, we must first identify which group we belong to, to do this, we categorise people.
- This might include categorising people based on religion, geography, ethnicity, political affiliation and so on.

Social identification
- Having categorised people (including ourselves) we then seek to identify with that group.
- We adopt behaviour traits associated with a particular group. For example, we might wave flags to express patronage to a country or wear certain clothing brands to denote membership of a particular social group.
- At this stage, perception of self-worth and esteem are inextricably linked to the group.

Social comparison
- Once we have categorised and identified with a group, we then compare and contrast with other groups that we do not belong to.
- To maintain self-esteem, the group to which we belong is seen as better than groups we do not belong to.
- It is at this stage where we are likely to witness prejudicial behaviour. Should two groups identify each other as rivals, they will compete for prestige, this is a competition of group identities, rather than a competition for resources.

Figure 2.6 Mental processes of social identity

the Bay of Pigs invasion (1961) and the Vietnam war (1964–1967), to group-think. Janis argued that in each of these cases, groupthink prevented alternative views from being expressed and subsequently evaluated on their own merits. Janis identified eight symptoms of groupthink, as illustrated in Table 2.3.

Later in this chapter, we look at examples of groupthink in action.

2.4.2.4 *Social identity and consumerism*

In post-modern society, a key driver to consumerism is social identity. Riesman's landmark book *The Lonely Crowd* (1950) is considered to have set the foundations for the sociological study of how we use consumption as a tool in which to present ourselves in the image of others. Riesman and his colleagues argued that there are three cultural stages which we progress through, from hunter-gatherers to post-modern economies, where social identity is an instrument of consumerism. Each stage is loosely determined by population growth, as illustrated in Table 2.4.

In post-modern society, consumption is not about the material worth of an object but about the symbols of identity associated with that object. Intuitively, we assume that our consumption behaviour helps to establish and sustain a sense of individuality. However, in post-modern societies, consumption is less about individualism and more about how we identify with our place in society and how we choose to project that identity. In other words, our consumption behaviour helps to establish and maintain social identity. It follows that to understand the determinants of consumption, we need to understand the concept of social identity in relation to consumption.

Table 2.3 Symptoms of groupthink

Symptom	Definition
Illusion of invulnerability	• Group members exhibit excessive confidence that can lead to risk-taking.
Collective rationalisations	• Group members ignore (or rationalise) thoughts or suggestions that challenge what is the perceived group consensus.
Belief in inherent morality	• Group members believe their actions are morally irreprehensible and ignore possible ethical or moral consequences of their decisions.
Stereotyped views of out-groups	• Group members hold prejudicial views about the out-group.
Self-censorship	• Group members fail to share perspectives that deviate from the perceived group consensus.
Direct pressure on dissenters	• Group members suppress views that are counter to the perceived group consensus.
Illusion of unanimity	• Group members assume that the majority view is unanimous.
Self-appointed mind-guards	• Group members protect the leader and the group from information that might challenge the perceived group consensus.

Table 2.4 Key cultural types and social identity

Stage	Definition
Stage 1: Tradition-directed culture	• There is considerable potential for population growth. • Behaviour is defined and given meaning by traditions of the past. • Values and social norms are drawn from our ancestors.
Stage 2: Inner-directed culture	• Although populations are growing, they have yet to reach density. • The emphasis is less on rules and traditions and more on how we choose to live with others in society, whereby our sense of self is about how we relate to wider society. • Values and social norms are drawn from immediate family, religion and society. • It is at this point where we witness the emergence of consumerism.
Stage 3: Other-directed culture	• Populations have grown to such an extent that there is density and some are in decline. • People are willing to accommodate others to gain approval, a behaviour key to maintaining order in complex societies that grew out of industrialisation. • It is at this point that consumerism becomes an instrument of social identity for most modern societies.

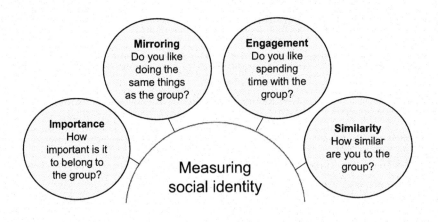

Figure 2.7 Key questions in measuring social identity

2.4.3 Measuring social identity in behavioural research

2.4.3.1 Quantitative measurement

In measuring social identity, it is important to ensure that the questions are tailored to the target group under consideration. There are broadly four core question areas to consider, as illustrated in Figure 2.7.

The 'about me' questionnaire (AMQ) has been used to measure aspects of self-identity in children and adolescents (Maris, 2002).

2.4.3.2 Qualitative immersion

Social identity can also be explored qualitatively, where the researcher can probe and explore the reasons behind the participants' responses in detail. Understanding why participants belong to a specific group will lead to a more detailed understanding of the nature of social identity. Conducting focus groups with specific groups will allow the moderator to observe how individuals from the group interact with each other and helps reveal the nature of social identity.

2.4.4 Social identity theory in action

2.4.4.1 'Us' and 'them' advertising

Marketeers that use the knowledge of the out-group to promote the in-group can create powerful marketing campaigns that appeal to our sense of self. Naturally, this requires a detailed understanding of the target audience in the first place.

Typically, this type of advertising highlights the negative aspects of the out-group and the relative positives of the in-group. For example, the Spanish car manufacturer Seat, ran the 'Because them, us' commercial in 2019 which is a call out to the target audience to reject the antiquated ways of the past and embrace a new enlightened future. Rather than following the well-trodden path of focusing on the virtues of the car, Seat looked to connect with a younger more progressive and liberal audience (the in-group). The advert used imagery to highlight negative connotations of the older more conservative baby boomer generation (the out-group), including fox hunting, owning art and traditional business practices. Each image is juxtaposed with more liberal versions and opposing statements that helped to distinguish the out-group from the in-group:

■ Because they did, we don't.
■ Because they won't, we will.
■ Because they own, we share.
■ Because they complicate, we simplify.
■ Because they judge, we embrace.
■ Because they look back, we look forward.

Another example of us and them advertising is McDonald's 2017 coffee advert that spoofed the hipster coffee culture. The advert shows customers in various artisan coffee shops struggling to deal with overly complicated and expensive coffee, and compares this to the ease of ordering and the affordability of the McCafé range. In this instance, the advert is appealing to those who want a simpler and more affordable coffee (the in-group) and suggesting that those wanting a complicated and expensive coffee should go elsewhere (the out-group).

2.4.4.2 Football hooliganism and tribal behaviour

Sadly, we are all too familiar with football violence and notwithstanding the efforts of FIFA (football's world governing body) to stamp it out, it persists in the domestic and national games. The drivers to football hooliganism are complex and heterogeneous, as illustrated in Figure 2.8.

Social identity is key to understanding football hooliganism (Gow and Rookwood, 2008; Knapton et al., 2018). With a strong club identity, tribal behaviour can occur, manifesting in highly ritualised behaviours, membership being awarded by proving oneself with antisocial behaviour or acts of violence against the opposing team's supporters. A sense of 'us' and 'them' is promoted, where the football club 'territory' is defended at all costs. Marginalisation and poor socialisation are also thought to be factors, where those that struggle to identify with society use football hooliganism as an outlet. Alcohol and drug use, the media, team

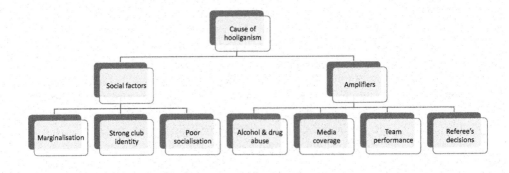

Figure 2.8 Causes of football hooliganism

performance and the decisions of the referee all serve to fan the flames of football hooliganism.

Below are examples of groupthink in action.

2.4.4.3 Attack on Pearl Harbour and misconceptions of the Japanese threat

One of the more infamous examples of groupthink is the attack by the Imperial Japanese Navy on the American naval base at Pearl Harbour in Honolulu, on 7 December 1941. The American navy had intercepted messages that made clear that the Japanese were preparing for an attack; nonetheless, the American navy was caught largely unaware on the day. Janis argued that this was a product of the following collective rationalisations and illusions of invulnerability:

■ The American pacific fleet was sufficiently strong to act as a deterrent to attack.
■ Japan would not attack, because it would bring America into a war that they would inevitably win.
■ Any attack would be spotted in good time and immediately repelled.

The strength of the above collective rationalisations and illusions of invulnerability (amongst others) was sufficient to prevent the senior command from considering alternative outcomes and not getting ready for the impending Japanese attack.

2.4.4.4 9/11 attacks and misconceptions of the threat of Osama bin Laden

A more recent example of groupthink is the Central Intelligence Agency's (CIA) failure to prevent the Al-Qaeda attacks on American soil on 11 September 2001.

It would not be unreasonable to argue that it is extremely difficult to predict a terrorist attack; however, the failure of the CIA might be, at least in part, a product of groupthink. The CIA is known for employing the 'best of the best' with only 1 in 20,000 applicants meeting the mark. As is often the case, those responsible for recruiting, chose candidates who were like themselves, and those they felt would be best placed to protect the American way of life. Inevitably, this resulted in a group of employees that broadly shared the same beliefs and values as their employers that were largely white, middle class and protestant; one might argue, an ideal environment in which to foster groupthink. Regarding Osama bin Laden, there was evidence of collective rationalisations, illusions of invulnerability and stereotyping:

- When Osama bin Laden made his declaration of war on America, it was from a cave in Tora Bora, eastern Afghanistan. Osama bin Laden was dressed in cloth and combat fatigues, with a beard down to his chest, given this, he was seen to be relatively primitive.
- Osama bin Laden often made proclamations in poetry, which was taken as evidence of eccentricity, in turn, helping to reinforce the perception that he was backward.
- There was a misguided belief that Osama bin Laden could not 'out communicate' the world's most advanced communications nation.

To a Muslim audience, it would have been immediately obvious that Osama bin Laden's attire was associated with holy prophets, yet this was missed by the CIA. The cave is a classic example of symbolism; Mohammed sought refuge in a cave when running from his oppressors in Mecca. For Muslims, poetry is not seen as eccentric, but indicative of something holy. So, the symptoms of groupthink within the CIA might well have resulted in the threat of Osama bin Laden not being taken seriously, yet all the signs were there to be seen.

2.4.4.5 Social media influencers and social identity

Social identity is a key component of social media marketing. We are all familiar with checking our social media accounts, streaming music and videos, whereby our online behaviour is familiar and omnipresent. In the online world, we have witnessed the advent of social influencers where video blogs from social influencers have become a common marketing tool on Instagram, Facebook, Snapchat, Twitter and YouTube. Social influencers generate conversations, encourage engagement and create cultural trends. As with the physical world, we follow people and join groups with similar interests, beliefs and values. We identify with social influencers, which helps reinforce our self-worth and esteem. When a social media influencer promotes/endorses a product in a social media group, it is likely that followers will purchase that product. This approach is exemplified by the retailer Boohoo, who in 2019 spent £80m on social influencers to help promote their products on social media (Denton, 2019).

2.4.5 Implications for behavioural research

1 Belonging to social groups is key to defining our sense of self and helps promote self-worth and esteem. We tend to look at the world as 'us' and 'them' and seek to support the identity of the groups we believe we belong to. In promoting the in-group, we adopt prejudicial views of the out-group. Researching social identity will tell us something about how participants see themselves and others in the social world.

2 Ownership of products helps support our sense of self-worth and esteem. We purchase products that we see as emblematic of the group we belong to.

3 Juxtaposing the in-group against the out-group can create a strong marketing hook, as illustrated by Seat's 'Because them, us' and McDonald's 'Hipster spoof café' commercials.

4 The emergence of social influencers makes clear the potential of using social identity to encourage brand identification and product purchase.

2.4.6 References/further reading

Gumplowicz, L. (1881). *Rechtsstaat und Socialismus [Legal state and socialism]*. Innsbruck, Austria: Wagner'sche Universitäts-Buchhandlung.

Gow, P., and Rookwood, J. (2008). Doing it for the Team – Examining the Causes of Contemporary English Football Hooliganism. *Journal of Qualitative Research in Sports Studies*, 2 (1), pp. 71–82.

Janis, I. L. (1972). *Victims of Groupthink: A Psychological Study of Foreign Policy Decisions and Fiascoes*. Boston: Houghton Mifflin.

Knapton, H., Espinosa, L., Meier, H., Bäck, E., and Bäck, H. (2018). Belonging for Violence: Personality, Football Fandom, and Spectator Aggression. *Nordic Psychology*, 70 (4), pp. 278–289.

Orwell, G. (1949; reprint, 2017). *1984. Penguin Book.*

Riesman, D., Glazer, N., and Denney, R. (1950; reprint, 2001). *The Lonely Crowd: A Study of the Changing American Character*. New Haven, CT: Yale University Press.

Sumner, W. (1906; reprint 2017). *Folkways: A Study of the Sociological Importance of Usages, Manners, Customs, Mores, and Morals*. Pantianos Classics.

Tajfel, H., and Turner, J. C. (1979). An Integrative Theory of Intergroup Conflict. In W. G. Austin, and S. Worchel (Eds.), *The Social Psychology of Intergroup Relations*, pp. 33–47. Monterey, CA: Brooks/Cole.

Below is a link to Boohoo's use of social influencers:

Denton, J. (2019). *Fast-Fashion Firm Boohoo Harnesses the Power of Celebrities and Social Media 'Influencers' to Enjoy Surging Sales.* This is Money, 25th April. https://www. thisismoney.co.uk/money/markets/article-6953983/Fast-fashion-group-Boohoo-harnesses-power-celebrities-enjoy-surging-sales.html [accessed 23/04/2021].

Below are links to us and them advertising:

McDonald's (2017). Hipster Spoof Advert. https://www.youtube.com/watch?v=Kra1e WAiKvE [accessed 23/04/2021].

Seat's (2019). Because Them, Us. https://www.youtube.com/watch?v=sAykd_FhWhQ [accessed 23/04/2021].

2.4.6.1 *Want to know more?*

If you wish to know more about social identity theory, then the original article by Tajfel and Turner is worth a read:

Tajfel, H., and Turner, J. C. (1979). An Integrative Theory of Intergroup Conflict. In W. G. Austin and S. Worchel (Eds.), *The Social Psychology of Intergroup Relations*, pp. 33–47. Monterey, CA: Brooks/Cole.

2.5 Symbolic interactionism: creating shared meaning through social interactions

2.5.1 *Defining symbolic interactionism*

Symbolic interactionism is a major theoretical perspective in sociology that originates from the pragmatist research philosophy. The theory is a framework in which to understand the relationship between the individual and society. According to interactionists, people behave based on what they believe to be true, that is, a subjective rather than an objective truth. The theory contends that through social interactions, meaning is created and negotiated. Social interactions rely on symbols that have shared meaning, such as words and gestures. Symbols have no obvious intrinsic meaning, rather, meaning is conferred by social actors. Earlier in this chapter, we discussed religion as an agent in which to facilitate socialisation and reinforce social norms in society. Interactionists would argue that our beliefs and experiences are not sacred unless individuals in society deem them to be so. The star of David (Judaism), the cross (Christianity) and the crescent and star (Islam) are all examples of sacred symbols, in which social interactions between religious leaders and followers help to affirm these symbols as sacred. Interactionists look at behaviour at a micro level, acknowledging that individuals have agency, making choices and exerting some sense of control over their lives. As we

Table 2.5 Three key premises in symbolic interactionism

Premise	Definition
Individuals act towards physical objects, actions and concepts based on the subjective meanings they derive from them.	• According to Blumer, the meaning of things is based on what we do with them. Take the colour red; in China, the colour is symbolic of good fortune and happiness. It is also used in celebrations, is a colour traditionally worn by brides and is thought to ward off evil. In western cultures, the colour red signifies danger. It is used to denote stop at pedestrian crossings. Phrases such as, 'caught red-handed', 'red rag to a bull' and 'red flag' further substantiate the colour red as a negative.
The subjective meanings we derive from physical objects, actions and concepts is a product of social interactions.	• It is assumed we have agency; we interact with each other based on the meaning we ascribe to physical objects, actions and concepts, rather than passively reacting to things. • Meaning is assumed to be a product of language and symbols we use to communicate. • Meaning is clear if there is consensus amongst social actors. If consensus is low, then the meaning will be ambiguous.
The subjective meaning of physical objects, actions and concepts is modulated through an interpretative process that allows us to process the things we encounter.	• This process involves an inner dialogue, akin to talking to ourselves, where we determine the meaning. • Role-taking is also important in aiding interpretation where we look at the perspective of others in social interactions.

will see in the various assumptions and concepts of symbolic interactionism discussed below, social interactions permit us to learn about ourselves and the social world we inhabit.

2.5.2 Reviewing symbolic interactionism theory

George Herbert Mead laid the foundations of what is now known as symbolic interactionism. He never published his work and it was only after his death that his former students published his theory and notes, in *Mind, Self and Society* (1934). Mead believed that the mind was a product of society and that society precedes the self. That is, we are born into societies that precede our existence and over time we learn to interact with society; we will return to this notion shortly. It is Blumer, a former student of Mead, who first coined the phrase symbolic interactionism. According to Blumer (1969), there are three key premises to the theory, as illustrated in Table 2.5.

Subjective meaning is a powerful determinant of behaviour, so much so, that objective truths can sometimes be ignored entirely. Take smoking amongst teenagers, teenagers are aware of the dangers to their health from smoking, yet some still smoke. Through social interactions with their peer group, some teenagers associate smoking with being cool; as such, by smoking, individuals are projecting a positive image to that group. In this instance, the symbolic meaning overrides the objective truth, that smoking is bad for your health.

Symbolic interactionalism is synonymous with theorising about the development of self; below, we look at symbolic interactionism's perspective on the development of self and the definition of situations.

2.5.2.1 The development of self

2.5.2.1.1 GEORGE HERBERT MEAD'S 'I' AND 'ME' AND THE GENERALISED OTHER

With agency at the heart of symbolic interactionism, the concept of self is not seen as a constant but evolving as a product of continual social interactions. As discussed, Mead assumed the society precedes the self. Further, Mead saw the self as inherently social in nature and drew a distinction between subjective and objective elements of self, referred to as the 'I' and 'me', respectively. The 'I' initiates action and is thought to be impulsive and spontaneous in nature. The 'me' is more reflective and is key to evaluating things. It is thought that we seamlessly move from 'I' to 'me', where an initial action becomes an object of reflection, where we look at our own behaviour and reflect on how we think others have judged that behaviour. Key to the 'me' part of self is the existence of social norms in the groups that we inhabit. As such, the 'me' is the arbiter of the 'I'. Social norms of the group and wider society are referred to as the 'generalised other'. The generalised other helps us understand the expectations people have of us. Key to the generalised other is role-taking, where we adopt the perspective of others in our social group. Mead used baseball as a metaphor for explaining the generalised other. In baseball, there are a set of defined rules for different roles on the field. It is important that individuals can adopt the perspective of other players on the field, along with looking at their own position as part of the wider team. This is a reflective act, where through our interpretation of other roles, we decide how best to behave in any given situation. This is just one example; it follows that there will be many generalised others based on different situations.

2.5.2.1.2 CHARLES HORTON COOLEY'S LOOKING GLASS SELF

The reflective nature of the self is best demonstrated by Cooley's (1902) concept of the 'looking glass self'. Cooley was a key figure in the origination of symbolic interactionism and was interested in how we perceive ourselves based on how others see us. For example, a student is tasked with making a presentation to the rest of the class, inevitably the student will be looking at their audience and observing communication between audience members. During this process, the student is interpreting and ascribing meaning to the audience's actions. In so doing, the student is defining who they think they are, based on other people's reactions to them. The looking glass self is not a direct reflection of how others see us but our perception of what we think other people think of us based on the information cues available. In other words, Cooley acknowledges that we do not know for certain how others feel about us. Further, Cooley argued that rather than simply accepting images of our self, we actively interpret them. That is, our interpretation of our perceptions of others allows us to form an appropriate response, such as pride if we feel that the audience liked our presentation, or embarrassment if we feel that the audience thought our presentation was poor in some way.

2.5.2.2 *Defining the situation*

2.5.2.2.1 ROBERT MERTON'S SELF-FULFILLING PROPHECY

Merton (1948) suggested that an expectation or prediction of something comes true because we believe it will, that is a self-fulfilling prophecy, which is a false definition of the situation. Social interactions are key to establishing this phenomenon, where language and symbols are used as labels to signify expectations. For example, the 2008 financial crash happened because of a collapse in the subprime mortgage market. Moreover, there was a self-fulfilling prophecy at play. Householders were faced with falling house prices that caused uncertainty. This was exacerbated by dire and downbeat news stories about the imminent collapse of the economy. Further, householders conversed with friends, family and neighbours who saw their homes repossessed by the banks. Consequently, householders sought to take remedial action to protect their positions. This included paring back expenditure and selling stocks and shares, which helped to create a financial contagion that spread across the markets around the world. To put this in perspective, economists from the Federal Reserve Bank of San Francisco argued that the demand effect of uncertainty resulted in at least a 1% increase in the unemployment rate in America (Leduc and Liu, 2012).

Stereotyping is a consequence of the self-fulfilling prophecy. For example, groups that are stereotyped as more intelligent, can in fact become more intelligent than those who are deemed less intelligent. A similar outcome occurs for those that are deemed more likeable than others. In these examples, individuals are not making judgements based on objective truths but based on what they believe to be true. It is perhaps worth noting that we do not rigidly subscribe to stereotypes but make judgements through social interactions. Nonetheless, stereotyping can lead to significant inequalities and prejudices, such as racism, ageism and sexism.

2.5.2.2.2 NAMING AND KNOWING

Naming things helps to define the situation, whereby names help to convey meaning. Typically, names are a form of shorthand for a fuller description of something. In naming a thing, the knowledge about it is important. Naming also helps to communicate the likely actions towards something. For example, imagine you are invited to a friend's barbecue, we know enough about the conventions of barbecues to assume with reasonable confidence it will be a social gathering where food is cooked outdoors. It will also be clear to us that it will be an informal event where we will be expected to dress casually, help ourselves to refreshments and food, and mingle with other guests. As such, the word barbecue acts as a repository of knowledge and expectations that direct behaviour.

2.5.2.2.3 IRVING GOFFMAN'S DRAMATURGICAL ANALYSIS AND IMPRESSION MANAGEMENT

Goffman (1956) argued that rather than a single self-concept, self is a product of different situations. Goffman used the theatre as an allegory for studying social interactions, where people in everyday life are like actors on a stage, playing a variety of roles. The audience are other people who observe the role you play and react to your performance. Performing helps to define the situation, by communicating what is expected of the performer and others, depending on whether they are front- or backstage:

- Frontstage: we are aware that others are watching us, and we abide by normative expectations that help to define how we interact with the audience. This includes what role we play and under what circumstances. Further, by acting/adopting roles, we attempt to present ourselves in the best possible light. For example, we might show deference to display respect or confidence to project a positive image of ourselves to the audience.
- Backstage: where no one is watching us, we are free from normative expectations. Further, backstage we can rehearse behaviours prior to trying them out front on the stage.

At the heart of Goffman's thinking is that we are constantly engaged in a process of impression management, where we attempt to present ourselves in the best possible light. In dramaturgical analysis, meaning is derived from the actions of the social actors rather than what they say, given this, emphasis is placed on non-verbal cues, such as facial expressions, body language and gestures. We return to the subject of nonverbal communication in Section 5.3.

2.5.2.3 Socialisation and reciprocity

Earlier in this chapter, we discussed the role of primary and secondary socialisation as a mechanism in which to internalise social norms and values. Structural sociologists suggest that primary socialisation is a one-way street where children are the recipient of the teachings of their parents. In other words, the child is seen as a passive recipient of the agents of socialisation. Symbolic interactionists see primary socialisation as a two-way street where children have some part to play in the socialisation process. For example, a parent seeks to exert control over a child, but the child responds by talking back or sulking, whereby the child is attempting to negotiate their position. During this process, both the adult and child are observing each other's behaviour through social interactions. As such, social-isation is seen as a dynamic and reciprocal activity between children and adults where together they influence the nature and outcomes of primary socialisation. In a similar vein, symbolic interactionists see secondary socialisation as a dynamic and reciprocal activity between social actors in different social environments. For example, a university student is about to take their final-year exams in modern history, and they acknowledge that it will not be possible to learn everything that has been taught and decide to focus on the content they expect to come up in the exams. Through social interactions with fellow students, it becomes clear that other students are adopting a similar strategy, resulting in a 'socialised response' to the problem. With the interactionist's emphasis on social interactions as the basis of socialisation, secondary socialisation is thought to be a continuous process.

2.5.3 Measuring symbolic interactions in behavioural research

2.5.3.1 Participant observation/ethnography

To locate and understand the subjective meaning of things, researchers will need to immerse themselves in the everyday activities of the individual and the social groups they inhabit. Given this, interactionists favour participant observation/ ethnography. In participant observation, there are essentially four stages, as illustrated in Figure 2.9.

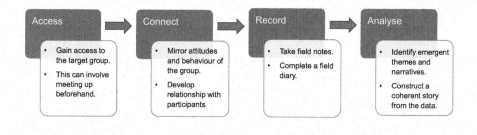

Figure 2.9 Key stages of participant observation

Building a bond with participants helps in seeing things through the lens of the participant and fosters a deeper understanding of the social situation. There are a few shortcomings to participant observation; the very presence of the researcher will influence the subjects under observation. There is also the chance that the researcher becomes deeply invested in the community under study and loses perspective and objectivity. On a practical level, this type of approach is very time-consuming, both in terms of conducting the field study and the analysis of the data.

An alternative approach is the use of online communities to observe social interactions and communication that signify symbolic meaning. In genuine online ethnography, the community members would not be aware of the researcher, whereby researchers will be able to interact with the participants as part of the community. Although not strictly ethnographic, the researcher could reveal themselves and opt to simply observe, thus addressing possible influence of the researcher on the group's behaviour.

2.5.3.2 Qualitative immersion

Qualitative techniques can also be employed to identify symbolic meaning. Asking participants to talk about how they think others see them, will help reveal the participant's reflections of self (albeit the researcher will no longer be at liberty to observe the context of behaviour, as would be the case with participant observation).

2.5.3.3 Discourse analysis

With language and symbols at the heart of meaning, discourse analysis tools should be considered as part of the researcher's toolkit. Textual and contextual analysis are the key forms of analysis, as illustrated in Table 2.6.

Table 2.6 Discourse analysis tools

Elements	Definition
Textual analysis: determining the composition and structure of discourse	There are two main analysis approaches to textual analysis: • Content analysis: involves breaking down the text into units of information for coding and categorisation. For example, the analysis might look for concurrent themes throughout the discourse. This involves identifying prevalence, time dedicated to themes and where and how themes intersect. • Semiotic analysis: involves identifying signs and their meanings. There are two components to signs. Signifiers that are physical signs such as letters, sounds and imagery. Signified are personal interpretations of physical signs and includes connotative (inferred), denotative (literal) and mythical meaning.
Contextual analysis: understanding the environment in which discourse occurs	There are two main analysis approaches to contextual analysis: • Situational analysis: involves looking at the circumstances in which the discourse originated, along with studying the social actors who originated the discourse. • Intertextual analysis: involves looking at the meaning of text based on other texts in relevant social spheres. This form of analysis assumes that individuals defer to other discourses to create their discourses. This process includes allusion, parody, quotation, appropriation and adaption. Intertextual analysis is useful in understanding the cultural and historical context of discourse.

On a cautionary note, discourse analysis is time-consuming and it is for this reason researchers tend to use one tool with only limited consideration for other tools that might help understand the data further. Time permitting, a blend of textual and contextual analyses should be employed.

2.5.4 Symbolic interactionism theory in action

2.5.4.1 American flag as a symbol of patriotism, or something more sinister

The American flag confers different symbolic meanings constituted by social interactions. For some, the flag is seen as a symbol of freedom and justice, and for others, a symbol of oppression. During the Trump presidency, the flag was used as an emblem of 'making America great again'. Consequently, many supporters of Trump adorned their homes with the flag. Such an act might be little more than a benign act of patriotism; albeit, Trump has a long history of racist commentary, including, referring to Covid-19 as a Chinese virus, calling Mexican immigrants criminals and rapists, and pandering to the white supremacist movement. Could it be a coincidence that far-right organisations began to place the American flag alongside the confederate flag? During the 'Black Lives Matter' demonstrations in America, it wasn't uncommon to see counter-protests from white supremacists brandishing the American flag, suggesting that the Black Lives Matter demonstrators were in some way un-American. In this instance, the symbolic meaning of the American flag changes, so much so, that the flag becomes a symbol of racism and intolerance.

2.5.4.2 Gender stereotypes

Naturally, gender is not determined by biology but is socially constructed. Boys and girls learn ways of behaving through interaction with parents, teachers, peers and the media. Notwithstanding the emergence of a more enlightened view of gender amongst younger more progressive and liberal generations, we still use male and female symbols as gender labels. These labels indicate gender roles and stereotypes that are ingrained in society. This can lead to harmful stereotypes, resulting in bias and inequalities.

2.5.4.3 Understanding the power of symbolism and college team support

Previously we looked at the importance of social identity in different settings. Cialdini et al. (1976) were concerned with how belonging to certain groups helps create a sense of self-worth and esteem. Specifically, Cialdini and his colleagues investigated whether we tend to bask in the glory of a group to improve our self-esteem. It was observed that students at American universities were much more likely to wear sweatshirts and other clothing, emblazoned with the university football's insignia, when the team won than when they lost. This study demonstrates how the symbolic meaning of the university's football insignia is used to help to enhance the student's self-esteem by associating with the success of the team.

2.5.4.4 Encouraging condom use in Africa

In the wake of the HIV/AIDS epidemic, extensive research has been conducted into ways in which to encourage healthy sexual behaviour in Africa, where the epidemic has had a devasting effect. Condom use remains the most effective way to abate the disease. However, campaigns to encourage condom use in Africa have had only limited success. Typically, campaigns focus on education to encourage

condom usage. Looking at condom use from the lens of symbolic interactionism might offer an alternative perspective. The symbolic meaning of condoms is
socially constructed through peer, family and community interactions. For example, condom use is more closely associated with family planning than the prevention of HIV transmission and other sexually transmitted diseases. Further, not
using a condom for a married couple is symbolic of closeness and intimacy, where
the introduction of condoms creates a sense of distrust between the couple (Heise
and Elias, 1995). In many African communities, HIV is considered a disease that
is a product of not subscribing to community morals, values and religious beliefs.
This can result in HIV stigmatism, where those with the disease report shame and
guilt and experience discrimination from those in their immediate community.
Further, in sub-Saharan Africa, HIV has been linked to witchcraft, where illness
is seen as a product of supernatural forces (Thomas, 2007, Bogart et al., 2011).
The shadow of years of apartheid also has a part to play, where some believe that
HIV is a disease created by white people to reduce black populations. The various
meanings ascribed to condom use and misconceptions about the causes of the
disease, provide a plausible explanation for the limited success of campaigns that
attempt to encourage condom usage through education. Reframing campaigns
to acknowledge the pervading norms and beliefs will help create more positive
associations with condom usage.

2.5.5 Implications for behavioural research

1 Symbolic interactionism is a major theory in sociology that provides researchers with a framework in which to understand the relationship between the
   individual and society. Symbolic interactionism provides researchers with a
   perspective in which to understand behaviour in everyday life where individuals are actively constructing and negotiating subjective meaning.

2 The notion of 'I' and 'me' is a simple mechanism in which to explain how
   the self develops through a process of continual social interactions. Instinctively, it seems we reflect upon our behaviour based on how we think others
   judge us.

3 The various theories about defining the situation clarify that definitions have
   consequences for behaviour. As such, understanding how people define the
   situation will help researchers better understand behaviour.

4 With an emphasis on social interactions, interactionists use participant observation to explore social reality. Whilst this approach ensures behaviour is
   observed in situ, it is time-consuming and presents issues of objectivity. Online
   communities, focus groups and one-to-one interviews are practical alternatives.

5 Textual and contextual analyses are also useful tools in understanding the
   composition, structure and context of language and symbols.

2.5.6 References/further reading

Blumer, H. (1969). *Symbolic Interactionism: Perspective and Method.* Englewood Cliffs: Prentice-Hall.

Bogart, L. M., Skinner, D., Weinhardt, L. S., Glasman, L, Sitzler, C., Toefy, Y., and Kalichman, S. C. (2011). HIV Misconceptions Associated with Condom use Among Black South Africans: An Exploratory Study. *African Journal of AIDS Research*, 10 (2), pp. 181–187.

Cialdini, R. B., Borden, R. J., Thorne, A., Walker, M. R. Freeman, S., and Sloan, L. R. (1976). Basking in Reflected Glory: Three Football Field Studies. *Journal of Personality and Social Psychology*, 34, pp. 366–375.

Cooley, C.H. (1902). *Human Nature and the Social Order.* New Brunswick, NJ: Transaction.

Goffman, E. (1956; reprint, 1990). *The Presentation of Self in Everyday Life.* London: Penguin.

Heise, L., and Elias, C. (1995). Transforming AIDS Prevention to Meet Women's Needs: A Focus on Developing Counties. *Social Science and Medicine*, 40 (7), pp. 931–943.

Leduc. S., and Liu, Z. (2012). Uncertainty, Unemployment and Inflation. *Economic Letter*, 17th September, 2012. Federal Reserve Bank of San Francisco.

Mead, G.H. (1934). *Mind, Self and Society.* Chicago, IL: University of Chicago Press.

Merton, R. K. (1948). The Self-Fulfilling Prophecy. *The Antioch Review*, 8 (2), pp. 193–210.

Thomas, F. (2007). 'Our Families are Killing Us': HIV/AIDS, Witchcraft and Social Tensions in the Caprivi Region, Namibia. *Anthropol Med*, 14 (3), pp. 279–291.

2.5.6.1 Want to know more?

The following book provides an overview of the key players in symbolic interactionism:
Meltzer, B., Petras, J., and Reynolds, L. (2015). *Symbolic Interactionism: Genesis, Varieties and Criticism.* London: Routledge.

2.6 Social practices: accounting for habitual behaviour

2.6.1 Defining social practices

Much of behaviour that is driven by social norms and social identity is habitual, where we carry out actions based on learnt social practices. In common parlance, a social practice relates to everyday activities that are typically routine or habitual in some sense. Going to work, preparing a meal, visiting the gym are all examples of habitual behaviour, where the emphasis is on a single action. In social practice theory, a practice or practices are composed of elements including resources, skills and cultural meaning. Importantly, social practices are inherently social, where through the performance of a social practice, elements of the practice are shared with society. This distinction will become clearer as we explore social practice theory in detail.

2.6.2 Reviewing social practice theory

2.6.2.1 Anthony Giddens' structuration theory

In the opening chapter, we discussed the debate amongst social scientists about the primacy of social structures and individual agency, in accounting for human behaviour. Some academics have questioned this dichotomous debate. Most notably, in *The Constitution of Society* (1984), the sociologist Giddens argued that activities that emerge are enabled by social structures, and at the same time, these structures are reinforced and legitimised by individual activity, which he referred to as a duality of structure. As such, there is a recursive relationship between social structures and individual agency, where primacy is given to neither; Giddens referred to this as structuration. Structuration theory looks at the processes that occur between social structure and individual agency. Specifically, in structuration it is argued that behaviour is enacted within the constraints of social structures, which includes rules that restrict and resources that enable individuals. Giddens identified three types of structures, as illustrated in Table 2.7.

The above structures exist not outside the individual, but embedded as memories, where the social actor will call upon knowledge about social structures to enable practices; moreover, in acting out practices, social structures are reproduced. Giddens distinguishes between practical consciousness and discursive consciousness and knowledge. Practical consciousness refers to knowledge the social actor has about a practice. Whereas discursive consciousness refers to the ability

Table 2.7 Structuration and social structures within knowledge

Structure	Definition
Legitimisation (rules)	• Refers to moral codes and standards, where an action is deemed legitimate based on known social norms and values.
Signification (meaning)	• Refers to how meaning is inferred through structures, where social actors call upon existing experience to infer meaning.
Domination (power)	• Refers to how power is used to control resources (allocative resources) and how social actors influence others (authoritative resources).

of a social actor to verbally express knowledge about a practice. Practical consciousness is semi-conscious and, consequently, non-reflective; in other words, knowledge about practices is largely taken for granted.

The premise of structuration is key to social practice theory, which contends that humans are agents who carry out actions based on social practices; in turn, the social world is negotiated and given meaning through practice by social actors.

2.6.2.2 Pierre Bourdieu's habitus

The sociologist, anthropologist and philosopher Bourdieu was key in bringing the idea of social practices into the purview of social science in the 1980s. Bourdieu suggested the concept of habitus, which refers to the physical embodiment of culture and includes ingrained social habits, skills and dispositions that guide behaviour (Bourdieu, 1984). Habits, skills and dispositions are ingrained to such an extent that they are second nature. Bourdieu used sport as a metaphor for habitus, where we have a 'feel' for the game. If we take cricket as an example, a batsman faced with a 90-miles-per-hour cricket ball will decide to play a defensive shot, a drive, a sweep or a flick based largely on gut feeling and intuition. Similarly, Bourdieu argues that we have a 'feel' for social settings, where we instinctively know how to behave based on ingrained social habits, skills and dispositions. For example, someone who grew up in a rough inner-city estate would have learnt how to avoid trouble and consequently will have a 'feel' for how to avoid trouble in other social situations. Bourdieu was particularly interested in inequality and the French social class system, and suggested that habitus included a taste for cultural objects, such as art. The French upper classes are introduced to art from an early age and consequently have learnt an appreciation for art that is culturally ingrained. In other words, the disposition for an appreciation of art is shared with people from similar backgrounds.

2.6.2.2 Elements of social practices

Social practices are defined by interdependent relationships between practice elements. There is some debate about the exact number and nature of elements. Reckwitz (2002) suggested seven elements of practice: body, mind, things, knowledge, language, structure and agent. Shove and colleagues drew upon Reckwitz's original conceptualisation and suggested a simplified model consisting of three elements that have come to be commonly cited (Shove and Pantzar, 2005; Shove et al., 2012), as illustrated in Table 2.8.

Social practice elements work as an interconnected system, where, for a social practice to occur all elements must be present and have some sense of concurrence. Cycling is often cited as an example of a social practice, as illustrated in Table 2.9.

Table 2.8 Social practice elements

Elements	Definition
Materials	• Physical objects that permit or facilitate activities to be performed in certain ways.
Competencies	• Skills and know-how that ensure or lead to activities being undertaken in certain ways.
Meaning	• Images, interpretations or concepts associated with a social practice that determine how and when they might be performed. • Meanings are shared and include social norms and identity.

Table 2.9 Cycling social practice elements

Elements	Definition
Materials	• Bicycle, cycle clothing, road network, cycle lanes and storage.
Competencies	• Fitness, skills needed to ride a bicycle, navigation and time management.
Meaning	• Shared meaning individuals have about cyclists. This can include, both positive and negative connotations. For example, cyclists might be thought of as aggressive road hogs or as champions of the environment.

Although social practices result in habitual behaviour, individuals actively negotiate and perform social practices in everyday life. Changes in any of the elements will change the nature of the social practice. For example, in England, the introduction of the London cycle hire scheme in 2010, made cycling more accessible. This change in the materials element resulted in an increase in short cycle journeys in the capital. Other material changes included the extension of the London cycle network, improvements in cycle storage and the introduction of speed limits to slow down motorists in cycle-danger hotspots. Regarding competencies, the introduction of cycle training/refresher courses helped to improve skills. Changing the meaning associated with cycling in London was also important. For example, many could reasonably argue that cycling in London is dangerous; therefore promoting improvements in road safety helps address these concerns and changes the meaning associated with cycling in London.

2.6.2.3 *Carriers of social practice*

Those that perform a social practice are referred to as 'carriers' of social practice. As noted, performance of a social practice is seen as an inherently social act, where carriers of practice help to reproduce socially learnt skills and cultural meaning. Whilst not dismissing the importance of individual agency, social practice theorists argue that rather than treating the social practice as a constant and looking for reasons why individuals perform social practices, the emphasis should be on what social practices ask of the individual and how social practices recruit carriers who are willing and able to perform a social practice. Naturally, it is not possible to perform every social practice as such; social practices must compete for resources. Further, not everyone can perform a social practice, where elements of social practice are not uniformly distributed, resulting in inequalities. It follows that rather than trying to understand why people conduct certain social practices, changing the social practice so individuals are willing and able to perform the social practice will help recruit carriers. Given the instinctive nature of social practices, the key to recruiting carriers is ensuring that performing social practices is effortless and efficient.

2.6.2.4 *Social practice networks*

A single social practice is not performed in a vacuum but is inextricably linked to other social practices in what might be termed a social practice network. If we return to the cycling example, the social practice of cycling to work is linked to the social practice of showering, where on reaching the office, we shower, change into our work clothes and pack our cycling clothes away. Further, when we get home, we will put our cycling clothes in the washing machine. As such, the social practice of cycling to our workplace is co-dependent on the social practices of showering and laundry. Although the notion of social practice network might seem a little nebulous (and it is often where criticism of social practice theory has been levelled), it does highlight the importance of understanding behaviour from the perspective of a network of interconnected social practices.

2.6.2.5 *Social practice decay*

The extent to which social practices are sustained relies on the continual performance of social practices through space and time. When there is no longer concurrence between elements or when one or more of the elements are no longer available, the social practice will decay or cease to exist. Sometimes, a practical substitute for an element is used to sustain the social practice. Elements from social practices that are no longer active either cease to exist or are repurposed.

For example, take the use of the withdrawing room, the meaning of a withdrawing room has largely been forgotten. The term is thought to date back to the 18th century and was a space in stately homes, where after dinner, the ladies would 'withdraw' into the withdrawing room, leaving the gentlemen at the dinner table to discuss business over a glass of port or brandy. This social practice ceased to exist as the social norms of women withdrawing after dinner slowly disappeared, upon which the withdrawing room is repurposed and becomes the drawing room.

2.6.2.6 Social practice theory and cultural theory

Social practice theory is often seen as an offshoot of cultural theory. This is understandable, given that many social practices are indistinguishable from cultural practices including:

- Religious acts or traditions.
- Rituals and festivals.
- Healthcare treatments.
- Musical tastes.
- Social distance and touch.
- Forms of artistic expression.
- Dietary preferences and culinary practices.
- Architectural design and construction.
- Childcare practices.

2.6.3 Measuring social practices in behavioural research

2.6.3.1 Qualitative immersion

With social practices as the unit of analysis, the research focus is not on individual agency or social structure but on the performance of social practices, over space and time. In social practice theory, there is no clear direction in terms of methodological approach. That said, qualitative techniques are often employed to explore how social practices emerge, how they are sustained and how they decay over time.

2.6.3.2 Quantitative and secondary data analysis

Assuming there is sufficient knowledge about a social practice, a quantitative approach can be employed. Additionally, secondary data sources can be used to trace how social practices emerge, how they are sustained and how they decay.

This form of analysis is useful in contextualising both qualitative and quantitative findings.

2.6.4 Social practice theory in action

2.6.4.1 Technology as a cultural enabler

Social practice theory is often considered in terms of the influence of technology on social practices and culture. For example, Shove and Southerton (2000) were interested in how the adoption of freezers in British households had become normalised in society over time. Shove and Southerton traced the evolution of the benefit of the freezer, from preserving home-cooked food to being part of a frozen food culture where the freezer is a key part of an efficient domestic economy and more recently in terms of convenience. The emphasis is not on individual attitudes towards the appliance but how the freezer has fundamentally changed domestic practices, particularly in removing many time-consuming domestic chores and encouraging women to enter the workforce.

2.6.4.2 Reducing bottled water consumption

More recently, social practice theory has been applied to everyday practices that impact on the environment. Most social practices require the consumption of energy, such as commuting to work on the train, preparing food and washing clothes. Researchers focus on how to transform social practices that are harmful to the environment. In 2007, the London on tap campaign was launched in partnership with the Mayor of London and Thames Water, to promote the consumption of tap water over bottled water. The environmental impact of glass bottles is significant, both in terms of the energy used to produce the bottle and to transport it. The campaign focused on the social practice of asking for bottled water in fine dining London restaurants, where generally patrons would be embarrassed to ask for tap water. To counter this normative behaviour, the campaign sought to present favourable conditions for ordering tap water in a restaurant. A competition was launched for the design of a new water carafe. The winning entry was 'tap top' by London based designer Neil Barron. The tapered design features four pouring spouts. For every carafe purchased by restaurants, a donation of £1 was made to Water Aid (a charity that campaigns for clean water around the world). Additionally, any patron who ordered a carafe of tap water could donate 50p to Water Aid. The net result was a fall in bottled water sales in participating restaurants. In this instance, the campaign helped to change all elements of the social practice of fine dining; the materials (water and carafe), competencies (dining out) and the meanings (social norms about ordering water in a restaurant). The success of this campaign has been replicated in other cities around the world.

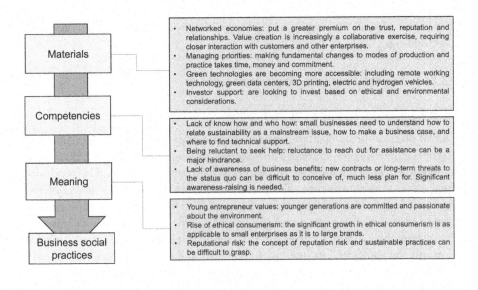

Figure 2.10 Social practices and small-business environmental behaviour

2.6.4.3 Encouraging small-business environmentally responsible practices

The practice of conducting business requires the consumption of energy which has an impact on the environment. It is generally acknowledged that business practices will need to evolve to address climate change. In this study, 1,000 interviews were conducted amongst small and large businesses, from a broad range of sectors, including those that have a significant environmental footprint, such as manufacturing and agriculture, along with sectors with a smaller environmental footprint, such as professional services. Social practice theory was used to identify ways in which to inform changes to social practices to help encourage sustainable behaviour in business, as illustrated in Figure 2.10.

2.6.4.4 Face coverings as a social practice

During the first wave of Covid-19, covering one's mouth and nose was positioned as a public health measure designed to reduce virus transmission. Consequently, discussions about mouth and nose covering centred on the efficacy of face-covering to reduce transmission. Van der Westhuizen et al. (2020) argued that face coverings should be reframed, not as a public health measure but as a social practice informed by social norms and expectations. In Asia, wearing face coverings is common and ingrained in the culture, reflecting the occurrence of respiratory disease outbreaks in the region. In many western societies, there is no precedent for such behaviour. Perhaps this explains the resistance to wearing face coverings by some. For example, in America, it has been suggested that insisting on wearing a face-covering is an infringement of civil liberties. In the United Kingdom, face mask wearing has not been universal; where it has been argued that the case for wearing a face mask is unproven, others are self-conscious and worry how they will be perceived by others. Van der Westhuizen and her colleagues suggest a narrative that is meaningful to the individual is required to encourage face coverings and create a widespread social practice, such as depicting wearers as altruistic and protectors of the community.

2.6.5 Implications for behavioural research

1   Much of our behaviour is habitual and can be explained by social practice theory. As such, social practice theory can be applied to behaviour in market research.

2   Considering social practices as a system of materials, competencies and meanings provides researchers with a framework in which to consider how to recruit individuals and groups to social practices. In principle, effecting change in any or all of the elements of social practice has the potential to change behaviour.

3   Social practices can be measured using qualitative and quantitative methods. Further, secondary data analysis provides rich contextual data about the emergence, evolution and decay of social practices.

2.6.6 References/further reading

Bourdieu, P. (1984). *Distinction: A Social Critique of the Judgement of Taste*. Cambridge: Harvard University Press.

Giddens, A. (1984). *The Constitution of Society*. Berkeley: University of California Press.

Reckwitz, A. (2002). Toward a Theory of Social Practices: A Development in Culturalist Theorizing. *European Journal of Social Theory*, 5 (2), pp. 243–263.

Shove, E., and Pantzer, M. (2005). Consumers, Producers and Practices: Understanding the Invention and Reivention of Nordic Walking. *Journal of Consumer Culture*, 5, pp. 43–64.

Shove, E., Pantzer, M., and Watson, M. (2012). *The Dynamics of Social Practice: Everyday Life and How It Changes*. Newbury Park, CA: Sage Publications.

Shove, E., and Southerton, D. (2000). Defrosting the freezer: From Novelty to Convenience - A Narrative of Normalization. *Journal of Material Culture*, 5, pp. 301–319.

Van der Westuizen, H-M., Kotze, K., Tonkin-Crine, S., Gobat, N., and Greenhalgh, T. (2020). Face Coverings for Covid-19: From Medical Intervention to Social Practice. *The British Medical Journal*, 19th August. https://www.bmj.com/content/370/bmj.m3021 [accessed 03/05/2021].

Chapter 3

How personality governs behavioural tendencies

CHAPTER OVERVIEW

Key theories: psychoanalytic theory, psychological types, adaptive unconscious, system 1 and 2 thinking, genetic epistemology, personal construct theory, trait theory, classical and operant conditioning and psychological behaviourism.

3.1 We begin by discussing psychoanalytic theory, where a distinction between the conscious and unconscious mind is made. We then consider contemporary views of the mind, including the adaptive unconscious and system 1 and 2 thinking.

3.2 Next, we look at personal construct theory and how we make sense of the social reality which is thought to define personality.

3.3 Personality trait theories are presented as a proxy for personality, and we look first at Allport and Cattell's trait theories, before turning to Eysenck's work in this field. Further, the big five personality trait theory is presented, along with dark trait dimensions and behaviour.

3.4 Finally, we look at classic and operant conditioning theories of behaviourism before looking at more contemporary behaviourist approaches to personality.

Introduction

Having considered theory that looks at social influence and behaviour, we turn now to personality as an antecedent of behavioural tendencies. As researchers,

 DOI: 10.4324/9781003169932-3

we must grapple with the notion of personality. Psychologists have spent decades formulating theories of personality, and the result is a fragmented and conflicting body of knowledge. Against this backdrop, the purpose of this chapter is not to exhaustively review all theories of personality, but to focus on theories that can be best applied to market research.

Why is personality important in behavioural research?

Before looking at different theories of personality, let us consider an intriguing paradox. Researchers are tasked with simplifying and ordering complex human behaviour. Inevitably, a reductionist approach results in a regression to the middle, the assumed normal, which can preclude researchers from gaining an appreciation of any underlying differences. Moreover, in the pursuit of understanding the complexity of personality, researchers can be prone to restricting their analysis to reporting the obvious, the known and the prosaic. The purpose of this chapter is to challenge this paradox and encourage researchers to think beyond similarities and consider differences where apparent.

In the beginning

Theories of personality can be traced back to humourism (a system of medicine detailing the composition and workings of the human body); although it is the Greeks, Hippocrates and Galen, who are credited with developing this into a medical theory. It was believed that certain human moods, emotions and behaviours were caused by an excess or lack of body fluids ('humours'), which were classified as blood, yellow bile, black bile and phlegm. Remarkably, this theory remained influential right up to the 1800s. In the early 1800s, Franz Gall developed the theory of phrenology, the study of bumps on the skull which supposedly revealed character traits and mental abilities. In its heyday, there were over 30 phrenological societies across Britain and many journals in both the United Kingdom and America devoted to its study. Although phrenology did help in focusing the field of neurology on the study of different cortical regions of the brain and certain mental functions, today, it is considered a pseudoscience and often associated with sexism, racism and eugenics. In this chapter, we start by looking at Freud and Jung's work on the unconscious mind. It is often thought that Freud was the first to come up with the notion of an unconscious mind. In fact, the term precedes Freud. Generally, it is thought that the phrase was first coined by the philosopher, Frederick Schelling in the 18th century, although discussions about the unconscious can be found as far back as 2500 BC in the Hindu text, Vedas.

3.1 Two minds: determining conscious and unconscious thinking

3.1.1 Defining the conscious and unconscious mind

Before Freud spoke about the unconscious mind, it was largely considered a taboo subject. The prevailing thought was that talking about the mental processes that people struggled to verbalise was unscientific. Fast forward to the present day, we now accept the existence of the unconscious, to the extent that it has become commonplace in our lexicon of language when discussing mental processes. In everyday life, we are faced with a myriad of information at any given time, and we simply do not have the conscious capacity to process all this information. It is thought the unconscious mind has evolved to address this problem and accounts for much of our everyday behaviour; it is instinctive, effortless, autonomic but subject to error on occasion. For more considered thinking, we rely on the conscious mind as it is reflective, deductive, requires more effort but results in fewer errors. We cannot have one without the other and as we will see, the unconscious and conscious mind serve different but complementary purposes.

3.1.1.1 Unconscious versus subconscious

Before looking at Freud's psychoanalytic theory, it is worth considering the terms unconscious and subconscious. Freud originally used the two terms interchangeably before settling on the unconscious to avoid confusion. In psychology, psychiatry and neuroscience, the term unconscious is typically used. However, it is not uncommon to see the use of the term subconscious, particularly in non-academic literature. In the absence of being able to draw a clear distinction between the unconscious and the subconscious, Freud's unconscious is used for consistency.

3.1.2 Reviewing conscious and unconscious mind theory

3.1.2.1 Sigmund Freud's psychoanalytic theory

Freud's psychoanalytic theory is one of the better-known approaches to personality, but also the least understood and, subsequently, often misquoted. Freud's theory was a product of continual development, and it originated with the topographical model, which distinguishes between the unconscious, preconscious and conscious mind. Freud (1915) likened the mind to an iceberg, in which most thought is unconscious and, consequently, submerged below the waterline, as illustrated in Figure 3.1.

The conscious mind is concerned with our awareness of thoughts in the moment and, consequently, the conscious part of the mind is above the waterline. Freud suggested that the conscious mind works closely with the preconscious.

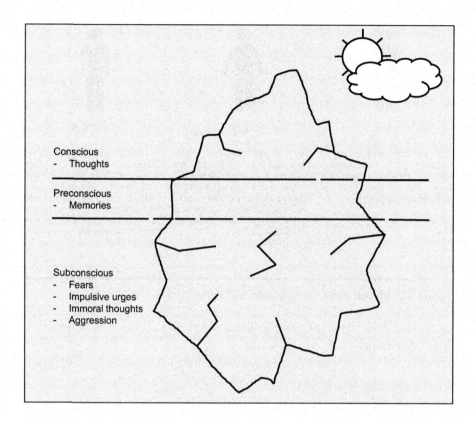

Figure 3.1 Conscious, preconscious and unconscious iceberg

The preconscious is concerned with memories that are accessible should the need arise. Consequently, the preconscious is just below the waterline. The unconscious is considered the most significant element of the mind and is a repository of thoughts that we are not aware of immediately. It is here where the motivations of behaviour are thought to be found, including fears, impulses, immoral thoughts and aggression. Freud argued that often these motivations are repressed or denied. Consequently, the unconscious is deep below the waterline.

Later, Freud (1923) developed a more structured model of personality, where there are three interrelated systems at play, namely, id, ego and superego, as illustrated in Figure 3.2.

3.1.2.1.1 A SYSTEM IN HARMONY

According to Freud, a prerequisite to a healthy personality is harmony between the three systems. If the ego successfully mediates between the impulsive needs

Id	Ego	Superego
Impulsive	*Rational*	*Moral*
Assumed to be unconscious. The id is focused on gratifying basic needs irrespective of the social consequences.	Assumed to exist in the conscious, preconscious and subconscious. The ego mediates between the id and superego, by focusing on meeting the needs of the id in an ordered and socially acceptable way.	Assumed to exist in the conscious, preconscious and subconscious. Values are learnt from parents, peer group and wider society. The superego works to suppress the urges of the id and attempts to make the ego act idealistically.

Figure 3.2 Id, ego and superego model of personality

of the id and the superego's desire for a just and perfect world, then the result is a well-balanced personality.

3.1.2.1.2 A SYSTEM IN CONFLICT

Should there be a conflict between the three systems, then there is potential for a maladjusted personality, and this can happen based on the following scenarios:

- If the id is dominant, then an individual will be inclined to act on primitive urges that might result in socially unacceptable behaviour.
- If the superego is dominant, then an individual will be inclined to be overly judgemental and unaccepting of all those that are not seen to conform to the exacting standards of the superego.
- If the ego is overly strong or weak, there will be disharmony between the id and the superego.

The inspiration for Freud's work was Anna O, a patient who was suffering from hysteria (i.e. paralysis, convulsions, hallucinations and loss of speech). Intriguingly, there was no obvious physical cause to the hysteria. It was thought that the hysteria was a product of trauma where the emotions associated with the trauma were not properly expressed. Dr Joseph Breuer (Freud's teacher) successfully treated Anna O, by making her aware of the meanings of her symptoms and in so doing, the unexpressed emotions were released and no longer needed to be expressed as symptoms. Although Freud saw himself as a scientist, his theories were based on case studies and as such, conformed to a subjectivist research philosophy.

3.1.2.1.3 PSYCHOSEXUAL THEORY

Freud believed that the primary motivating force behind human behaviour was sexual gratification. This is the more contentious part of Freud's theorising. Freud went on to argue that the development of personality is shaped by three core psychosexual stages, namely, oral, anal and phallic, where the unconscious is a collection of unfulfilled sexual desires. This part of Freud's theory falls outside the remit of this book. If you wish to read more about Freud's psychosexual theory, then most psychology textbooks on personality theory will address this.

3.1.2.2 Carl Jung's psychoanalytic theory

Jung was a protégé of Freud. They had a shared interest in the unconscious, with Freud considering Jung the heir apparent to psychoanalytical theory. Freud's deliberations about the unconscious as a collection of unfulfilled sexual desires did not sit well with Jung. Over time, Jung became critical of the emphasis on infantile sexuality and went on to develop his own strand of psychoanalytic theory.

Jung had an interest in all things religious, mythical and philosophical. This does help to explain some of the thinking behind Jung's theory, particularly the collective unconscious (Jung, 1933). Like Freud, Jung divides the human psyche into three core elements, as illustrated in Table 3.1.

Table 3.1 Human psyche elements

Elements	Definition
Ego	• The ego is at the very heart of consciousness. • Jung saw the conscious mind as a collection of thoughts, memories and emotions that a person is aware of. • A point of difference with Freud; there is no mention of instincts.
Personal unconscious	• Includes anything which is not presently conscious but could be in principle. • The personal unconscious is formed from individual experiences and includes memories that can be recalled and ones that are suppressed or forgotten.
Collective unconscious	• The most notable difference between Freud and Jung is the collective unconscious. • The collective unconscious is a level of unconsciousness shared with society, including latent memories from our ancestral and evolutionary past. • Our primitive past becomes the basis of the human psyche, directing and influencing present behaviour. For example, a fear of the dark, heights, snakes or spiders are all thought to be drawn from our primitive past.

Jung argued that the content of the collective unconscious is made from a set of archetypes (Jung, 1947). Jung suggests there are many archetypes, but placed particular emphasis on the following core archetypes:

Persona: begins as an archetype but at the point in which it is fully developed, it resides in the consciousness. This is the public face (or mask) we present to the world. It is driven by our desire to present a positive image of ourselves. Naturally, we can present a false impression to others, should we so choose.

Shadow: derives from our primitive animal past and is concerned with survival and reproduction.

Anima/Animus: is about the physical gender of our psyche. Jung believed as we begin our social lives as infants, and we are neither male nor female. Over time, society moulds us based on established norms and stereotypes of gender. The anima is the female aspect of the collective unconscious of men. The animus is the male aspect of the collective unconscious of women.

Self: according to Jung, the goal of life is to fully realise the self, where all aspects/determinates of our personality are expressed equally. Self is seen as a spiritual version of the body's homeostasis system; to achieve a state of 'selfhood' one would be neither good nor bad, neither ego nor shadow, neither conscious nor unconscious and so on.

Archetypes are a result of our collective experience and are thought to be personified by mythology. For example, reflecting thinking of the day, Jung suggested the mother/carer role as an archetype. Given our ancestors had mothers, our understanding of the mother/carer role is ingrained. Jung argued that women are born ready to want to be a mother, so seek out that role. The mother archetype is immortalised by primordial/earth mother mythology. As such, archetypes are spiritual rather than biological in nature. Typically, these archetypes are grouped into four broad categories, freedom, stability, belonging and mastery. In Figure 3.3, some of the other archetypes that are thought to exist in the collective unconscious are detailed.

Jung's theory of the conscious and unconscious mind was not as popular as Freud's. This is probably because Freud's theory is a lot less abstract than Jung's spiritual notion of the human psyche. Yet archetypes are self-evident in contemporary culture. It is possible to identify archetypes in different media sources. For instance, in the movie industry, there continue to be examples of storytelling that portrays conflict and struggle that help teach us the difference between right and wrong, good and evil, just as Jung had originally envisaged the role of archetypes in the collective unconscious.

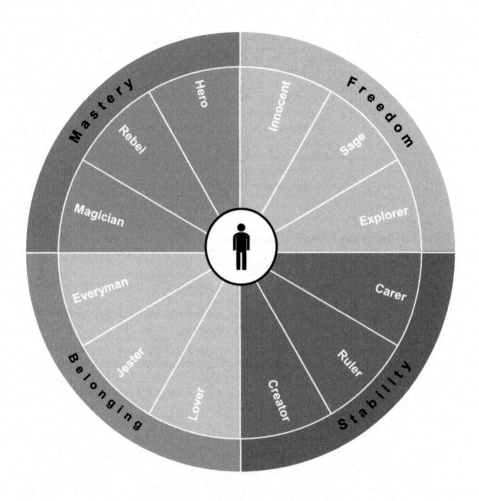

Figure 3.3 Carl Jung's 12 archetypes

3.1.2.2.1 CARL JUNG'S PSYCHOLOGICAL TYPES

Whilst Jung's notion of the unconscious mind was not as well received as Freud's theorising, Jung put forward a theory of personality types (or psychological types) that continues to be influential today. Jung was one of the first to popularise the notion of extroversion and introversion as key determinants of personality. Jung referred to extroversion and introversion as opposing attitudes, as detailed in Table 3.2.

Additionally, Jung suggested there are two judging functions (thinking and feeling) and two perceiving functions (sensation and intuition) that help us make

Table 3.2 Jung's psychological attitudes

Psychological dimensions	Definition
Extroversion vs. introversion	• Extroversion: reflects a preference for stimulation from the environment 'the outer world'. The extrovert is typically seen as social and seeks out the company of others. • Introversion: reflects a preference for stimulation from our inner mental state 'the inner world'. The introvert is typically seen as reserved and contemplative.

Table 3.3 Jung's psychological functions

Psychological functions	Definition
Opposite ways of judging Thinking vs. feeling	• Thinking: is a preference for analysis based on logical inference. • Feeling: is a preference for analysis based on subjective meaning.
Opposite ways of perceiving Sensation vs. intuition	• Sensation: is a preference for perceiving the world based on what individuals can see, hear, touch and taste. • Intuition: is a preference for perceiving the world through abstract concepts and theories.

sense of the world. The judging functions are decisive but can be rigid, whereas the perceiving functions are more flexible and interpretive in nature. The functions operate as opposing forces (or dichotomies) as detailed in Table 3.3.

3.1.2.2.2 DOMINANT ATTITUDE AND FUNCTION

It is thought that whilst we use all functions, only one function of the perceiving or judging dichotomies can be dominant at any one time (Jung, 1971). Further, Jung suggested that in addition to the dominant function there will be an auxiliary function, that is, a function from the non-dominant pair, that has a secondary influence on personality. Finally, the inferior function is the function opposite to the dominant, as illustrated in the examples below.

Example 1:

- ■ Dominate function: intuition.
- ■ Auxiliary function: thinking or feeling.
- ■ Inferior function: sensation.

Example 2:

- Dominate function: thinking.
- Auxiliary function: sensation or intuition.
- Inferior function: feeling.

The extroversion or introversion attitude dictates whether there will be an outer- or inner-world focus.

The dominant attitude and function will be in the consciousness, whilst the opposite attitude and function will be repressed in the unconsciousness. For example, if the function thinking and the attitude extroversion are dominant then the function feeling and the attitude introversion will be repressed in the unconscious mind. Repressed attitudes and functions might result in compensatory behaviour as the individual seeks harmony.

Based on the notion of a dominant attitude and function, Jung identified eight personality types:

- Extraverted thinking.
- Introverted thinking.
- Extraverted feeling.
- Introverted feeling.
- Extraverted sensation.
- Introverted sensation.
- Extraverted intuition.
- Introverted intuition.

With an emphasis on dominant attitudes and functions, Jung's theory is not strictly a model of personality type, but a measure of tendencies of consciousness. Later, we look at the Myer-Briggs-Type-Indicator as a psychometric tool with which to measure Jung's psychological types.

3.1.2.3 Adaptive unconscious

Whilst contemporary theorising about the unconscious mind owes much to the earlier work of Freud and Jung, how academics see the unconscious mind now is far removed from Freud's repressed unconscious and Jung's mystical collective unconscious. Psychologists were slow to take the unconscious mind seriously, largely because there was no objective measure of this part of the mind. With the emergence of cognitive psychology in the mid-1950s, it became clear that the unconscious is important for many mental processes, including learning, decision-making and making judgements. The unconscious is adaptive, having evolved to help us cope with the demands of modern-day life. The adaptive unconscious is thought to be instinctive, effortless and autonomic. That is, our cognitive processes have been made more efficient to ensure we can quickly carry out mental activities. To put this in context, imagine if we had to consciously consider every aspect of our speech, it would make social interactions very slow and cumbersome. Our adaptive unconscious has evolved to process language with relative ease and ensure that we have the capacity for other mental processes.

3.1.2.4 Introspection illusion

The introspection illusion is a cognitive bias where we wrongly assume that we have access to unconscious thought. This type of cognitive bias is best illustrated by the work of the psychologist Timothy Wilson. Wilson and his colleagues were concerned with whether introspecting about the choices we make post hoc, reduces satisfaction with that choice. Wilson conducted a study into how individuals rationalise their responses when choosing a poster to take home (Wilson et al., 1993). In this study, participants were randomly assigned to one of two groups:

- ■ Group one: presented with two posters and asked to choose one of the two posters to take home. Participants were then asked to discuss their choice.
- ■ Group two: presented with two posters and asked to choose one of the two posters to take home. Participants were not asked to discuss their choice.

Participants were contacted three weeks later and asked to state how satisfied they were with their poster choice. Those that had originally discussed their choice tended to be less satisfied than those who simply made a choice. This would suggest that group one had made a bad decision on the day. However, when participants attempted to make sense of their original decision, they tended to focus on attributes of the stimulus that were easy to articulate, rather than the root cause of their choice in the first place. Focusing on these attributes, unsurprisingly, results in a different evaluation of the stimulus, in this case, resulting in dissatisfaction with the choice made three weeks earlier. It seems we do not have access to all the decision influences in our unconscious, given this, we construct a narrative that provides us with a plausible explanation for behaviour. Curiously, we are not aware we are 'making things up'.

3.1.2.5 Two systems of thinking

Next, we look at the research into autonomic processing, which has come to dominate theorising on the unconscious in the last few decades. Neuroscientists and psychologists have converged on the idea of two systems of thinking, one which is intuitive and automatic and another that is reflective and rational; these types of thinking are referred to as system 1 and 2 thinking, respectively. A summary of the two systems is presented in Figure 3.4.

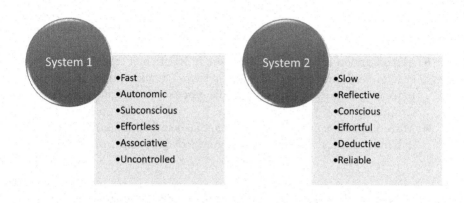

Figure 3.4 System 1 and 2 thinking

Kahneman (2011) described system 1 and 2 thinking, as fast and slow systems, respectively. System 1 is autonomic, hence fast, whereas system 2 is reflective, hence slow. It is thought that most of the time we rely on autonomic thinking and only when we get into difficulty, do we call upon reflective thinking. If we take the example of the multiple 4 × 4, then we can relatively easily deduce that this is 16; it requires little attention, whereby we can rely on autonomic thinking. If we change the multiple to 19 × 19, then the task becomes more complex, requiring the attention of reflective thinking.

The autonomic system can be trained although this takes practice. Take learning to drive a car; when we start out, the autonomic system has no experience of such a task, and consequently, it requires considerable attention to learn how to drive. Once we have begun to learn, some of the simpler tasks of driving can be taken over by the autonomic system. Upon passing our test, we have become reasonably competent drivers and are no longer reliant on system 2 thinking. Consider someone who drives to work and back each day; assuming it is the same route and uneventful, we are unlikely to be able to recall much of the journey. In this instance, we are relying largely on reflective thinking.

Given its simplicity and logic, system 1 and 2 thinking has been widely adopted. Indeed, this dualistic explanation of the human mind has transcended its academic origins and entered popular culture. Perhaps unsurprisingly, a few misconceptions have surfaced:

- Misconception 1: system 1 and system 2 thinking can be assigned to either side of the brain. Different regions of the brain are associated with certain mental tasks, but the notion of a right- and left-brain divide is unfounded. This misconception is probably a product of a belief that individuals are either left- or right-brain dominant (left-brain dominant is assumed to result in analytical thinking and right-brain dominant is assumed to result in more creative thought), a notion that can be traced back to the 1960s, that persists to this day.

■ Misconception 2: the two systems work in isolation of each other. The two systems work in tandem, in which, system 1 thinking frees up cognitive processing capacity to deal with mental processes that might require system 2 thinking.

■ Misconception 3: only in system 1 thinking do mistakes occur. Errors occur in both systems, although they are more likely in system 1 thinking.

3.1.3 Measuring the conscious and unconscious mind in behavioural research

The conscious mind is accessible, and we can use direct questioning to address conscious thinking; the same approach will be ineffective when delving into the unconscious mind. To better understand the unconscious mind, researchers need to frame questions in such a way as to gain access to the unconscious mind. Below, we look at several interview techniques that have proven effective in helping researchers locate and understand more deep-seated unconscious thought.

3.1.3.1 Laddering and means-end chain analysis

Laddering is a technique that has its origins in clinical psychology where it was first used to understand a patient's values and beliefs. In market research, laddering is a tried and tested technique, typically used to encourage participants to reflect upon their decision-making. The technique has been aligned to means-end-chain analysis to provide a working framework in which to understand purchase behaviour (Reynolds and Gutman, 1988). The theory contends that there is a hierarchy of drivers to purchase behaviour, ranging from the basic product attributes to core values, as illustrated in Figure 3.5.

In the example presented in Table 3.4, the moderator is seeking to establish what are the core values of purchasing a car. The moderator will start with a

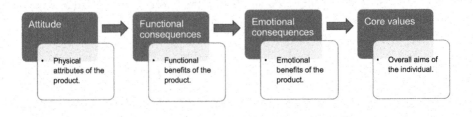

Figure 3.5 Drivers to purchase

Table 3.4 Moderator and participant dialogue

Individual	Dialogue	Comment
Interviewer	What is it about the car that led you to purchase it?	
Participant	I liked the colour and it is fast.	*This response tells us about the physical attributes of the car. The moderator then moves on to probe about the functional consequences.*
Interviewer	Why was the colour of the car important?	
Participant	Not many cars are that colour, most cars are silver, I wanted something that was a bit different.	*The 'why' helps us understand the reason for not wanting a silver car.*
Interviewer	Why is it important not to have a car that looks like all the other cars on the road?	
Participant	I like to be seen as a little different. My friends all think I'm a bit odd like that...	*The 'why' helps to elicit responses that reveal more about the person's emotions and values.*
Interviewer	And why is this important to you?	
Participant	I guess, it makes me feel good about myself.	*The 'why' helps to elicit the deep-seated driver to the purchase.*

general question to initiate conversation, and then ask questions about the functional and emotional drivers before focusing on core values.

On a cautionary note, it might take more than three or more questions to progress from the physical attributes to core values. Depending on the participant and the subject matter at hand, there might be a need for further qualifying questions at each stage. This can make the technique a little tedious for participants. Further, it must be acknowledged that later questions can be challenging to answer and it is important not to push for an answer when an answer is not forthcoming. Notwithstanding this, laddering can be applied to just about any research question and with skilful interviewing, is an effective technique to discover and understand unconscious thought. If you are not familiar with this technique, it is advisable to do a few practices to get comfortable with this line of questioning, and whenever possible, mix up the questions so the experience for the participant is less tedious.

3.1.3.2 *Projective techniques*

Projective techniques use symbolism and imagery to identify underlying beliefs, values and emotions, that reside in the unconscious mind. In Table 3.5, the most common techniques are presented.

Table 3.5 Projective techniques

Technique	Content
Personification	• Asking participants to make human-like associations about inanimate objects is a common technique used in branding research. • Participants are asked to say what type of personality comes to mind when thinking about a specific brand. • Alternatively, participants are asked to build a persona for a particular brand or product with the use of pictures and words.
Expression	• Participants are asked to express how they feel about a brand, a product or a situation, by painting, drawing or acting. • Although caution must be accorded, the outcome can say more about the participant's artistic abilities than about how they feel.
Creation	• Participants are presented with a picture of a person in a particular setting and then asked to construct a story about that person.
Completion	• Participants are asked to complete a task, such as complete unfinished sentences or add detail to a picture or a scene.
Role play	• Role play is a technique that involves asking participants to place themselves in someone else's shoes. For instance, participants might be asked to imagine they have been appointed head of marketing for a new online clothing brand and instructed to create a marketing strapline to launch the brand.
Withdrawal	• Participants are asked to stop using a product for a while and then instructed to complete an online diary/blog to share their feelings. • Withdrawal can also be used as a prioritisation task, where participants are asked to imagine a product as a hot air balloon which is weighed down with too many product features, participants must decide which features to jettison to ensure the balloon can rise.
Bring an item	• Asking participants to bring an item that has some relation to the research question can be a useful mechanism in which to understand participant's beliefs and values. For instance, participants might be asked to bring an item that helps them explain how they feel about a product or service. It is interesting to understand why participants chose that item in the first place.

3.1.3.2.1 PERSONIFICATION – THE BRAND PARTY

Let us now look at an example of personification. When understanding advocacy towards a brand, typically, our perceptions and beliefs about a brand are not immediately obvious. The brand party is a technique designed to go deeper and access unconscious thinking about brands. For example, participants are asked to imagine that the following brands are invited to a party, M&S, Waitrose, Morrisons, Aldi, Lidl and Tesco. Participants are then asked to consider how each brand would behave at the party. Questions might include:

- Who would turn up late?
- Who would talk to whom?
- Who would hog the limelight?
- Who would be a shrinking violet?
- Who would drink too much?
- Who would leave with whom?
- Who would get a taxi home?

The outcomes from the above questions help researchers get beyond the surface level knowledge and go deeper in exploring how participants feel about different brands. The upside of this type of technique is that not only can participants rely largely on the unconscious to answer the above questions but that the task is enjoyable, which helps keep participants engaged.

Like laddering, projective techniques are time-consuming to administer, so make sure you have allowed for this in your research. Moreover, it requires a certain degree of skill to be able to make sense of the outcomes of these types of techniques whilst avoiding possible interpretation bias. Nonetheless, when administered in the right setting, projective techniques are effective in connecting with deep-seated beliefs and values of the unconscious mind.

3.1.3.3 Myer-Briggs-type-indicator

As noted earlier, Jung's personality types are measured using the Myer-Briggs-Type-Indicator (MBTI). The indicator is one of the better-known measures of personality type. The test is used by universities and businesses worldwide. On a lighter note, even Disney princesses and Star Wars characters have been classified using the test. The measure is a self-reported introspective questionnaire. As discussed, Jung identified eight personality types based on the perceiving and judging functions, mediated by extroversion and introversion attitudes. When the measure was first developed in the 1950s, by Isabel Briggs Myer and her mother Katherine Briggs, perceiving and judging were treated as separate opposing functions, which resulted in 16 personality types.

3.1.4 Conscious and unconscious mind theory in action

3.1.4.1 Public relations and emotional unconscious

Freud's three systems of the mind have been used to inform public relations. One of the earliest exponents of this approach was Edward Bernays, a nephew of Freud. Bernays was a pioneer in public relations in the early to mid-20th century and applied Freud's psychoanalysis theory to consumer marketing. Most notably, the Lucky Strike 'Torches of Freedom' campaign was designed to appeal to the emotional unconscious, rather than the more rational consciousness. Bernays consulted Dr A. A. Brill, a psychoanalyst, who suggested that women saw smoking as an emblem of male power. In the early 20th century, women smoking in public was a social taboo, and it was associated with 'fallen' women, with movies portraying women smokers as 'sly' and 'devious'. To address this, Bernays created a counter-narrative of female empowerment, by linking smoking to marches for women's rights. In 1929, Bernays encouraged women to march down Fifth Avenue, in New York during the Easter parade, to protest against sexual inequality. Additionally, Bernays paid women to openly smoke Lucky Strike cigarettes in public, during the parade. Before the march, Bernays informed the press to expect women to light up 'torches of freedom' as a symbol of female empowerment. This seemingly scandalous behaviour attracted considerable press coverage and helped to make an association between Lucky Strike cigarettes and women's emancipation. The campaign was a huge success, resulting in a significant uplift in Lucky Strike sales.

Let us now look at examples of marketing that plays to the id, ego and superego.

3.1.4.2 Id, ego and superego advertising

3.1.4.2.1 ID ADVERTISING: ADDRESSING INSTINCTIVE NEEDS

Id advertising is designed to address an instinctive need. For instance, an advertisement that promotes perfume will often make an association between the perfume and a sense of glamour and beauty. Advertisements for chocolate and ice cream work in a similar way, where they are designed to appeal to our instinctive desires.

3.1.4.2.2 EGO ADVERTISING: ADDRESSING REALITY

Many sports brands use advertising that appeals directly to the ego, most notably, Nike, Puma and Adidas. Interestingly, this type of advertising looks to position a product or brand as an enabler to success, rather than focusing on the consumer using the product because of their success. Nike is one of the key exponents of ego advertising, where the brand is focused on building the customer's ego. Typically, Nike's advertising focuses not on Nike's products but on the consumer's desire to succeed. Examples of this include the following straplines: just do it, you gotta work hard to win, and you gotta want it. In these examples, whilst there is no explicit link between the brand's product and success, there is a subliminal association between being successful and being part of the Nike success story.

3.1.4.2.3 SUPEREGO ADVERTISING: ADDRESSING MORAL VALUES AND JUDGEMENTS

Advertising that appeals to our moral compass plays to the superego. This type of advertising encourages socially and culturally appropriate behaviour. This might include charity donation appeals, where messaging builds a link between individual behaviour and effect.

3.1.4.3 Retail brand values

Jung's 12 archetypes can be used to decode brand values. In Figure 3.6, Jung's archetypes are applied to high street and online retail brands. In this example,

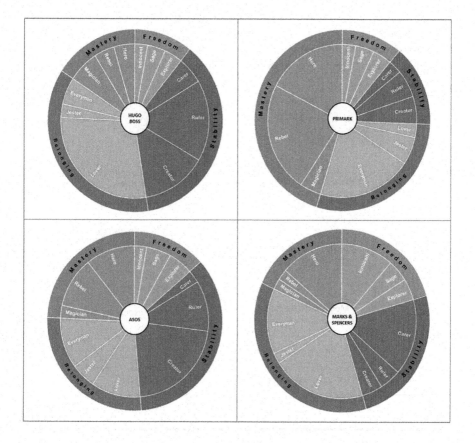

Figure 3.6 Carl Jung's 12 archetypes and retail brand values

participants were given stimulus cards for each archetype and then asked to place the archetypes next to the brand they felt best personified that brand. For each brand, scores were obtained by archetype.

3.1.4.4 Phishing and system 1 and 2 thinking

Phishing is a cybercrime where individuals are sent an email or text message masquerading as legitimate, but with the intention to gain access to their personal information. A phishing email or text will direct the recipient to a fake website and ask them to enter passwords and other sensitive information to gain access to their bank account or credit card details. In this study, qualitative research was conducted amongst consumers who had fallen foul of cybercrime. The purpose of the research was to identify the mental processes that occur during this type of event, with a view to developing support to minimise the impact of phishing and other forms of cybercrime. The results are presented in Figure 3.7.

In the first instance, consumers panic and faced with stress of the moment, default to system 1 thinking, typically shutting everything down. It is only after the immediate moment has passed do consumers then draw upon the resources of system 2. That is, they reflect upon the problem and attempt to seek a solution.

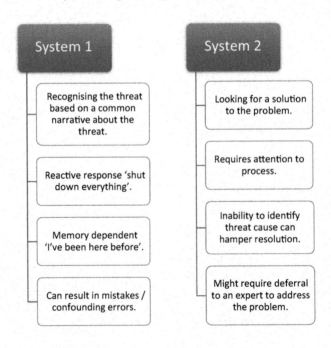

Figure 3.7 Phishing and system 1 and 2 responses

This study suggests that to help consumers deal with phishing, information and support must be directed to system 1 thinking in the first instance.

3.1.4.5 Understanding behaviour during the London King's Cross fire

On 18 November 1987, a fire broke out in the London Underground's King's Cross station ticket hall, killing 31 people and injuring a further 100. A public inquiry was launched to ascertain the cause of the fire. It was thought that a lit match fell through a wooden escalator and set fire to litter beneath it. Psychologists at the University of Surrey reviewed the statements of survivors (Donald and Canter, 1992). When the fire broke out, it quickly spread to the ticket hall. Virtually all the survivors headed back to where they had first entered the station or continued with the journey, rather than taking the route which would get them to the surface quickest (even when there were London Underground staff directing the public out of the station to safety). Given there is nothing to suggest that survivors behaved any differently than those who tragically lost their lives, it was concluded this behaviour cost lives. A likely explanation for this behaviour is in the stress of the moment, individuals deferred to system 1 thinking. This resulted in an autonomic response, where people defaulted to the existing travel scripts, which meant either continuing with their journey or heading back to the entry point. The outcome of this research underlined the importance of ensuring that appropriate measures are in place to help people make informed decisions in times of immense stress and uncertainty.

3.1.4.6 Harnessing the unconscious mind as a performance tool

In professional sport, psychologists work alongside coaches, physiotherapists and nutritionists to support athletes. Sports psychologists look at ways in which to harness the mind to unlock potential. Part of this is using the unconscious mind as a performance tool. For instance, if an athlete is trying to perfect the hurdles, by shaving a few milliseconds off their performance, they will naturally focus on specific tasks, including the lead and trail legs and the number of steps between hurdles. This inevitably requires conscious thinking, initially, where performance will not be at its best. Conscious thinking results in hesitation, nervousness and unnecessary muscle use, which slows down the athlete's movement. Every action in sport must be learned so it is a habit that requires little if any, thinking, beyond a few technical adjustments in the moment. Once learned, the unconscious can take over, resulting in effortless and in this instance, natural hurdling. As soon as the conscious mind comes into play, it no longer looks effortless and mistakes creep in. Additionally, athletes are encouraged to stay in the present and not focus on winning, which is somewhere in the future; thinking about winning requires conscious thought. If you were to ask the American athlete Aries Merritt what he remembers about setting a world record for the 110 metres hurdles at the London Olympics in 2012, he would remember little of the race but would recall running over the finish line ahead of all the other athletes. In other words, Aries relied almost entirely on the unconscious to get to the finish line and only then did the conscious mind come into play.

3.1.5 Implications for behavioural research

1 Freud and Jung invite us to question the notion of the rational economic man, making rational decisions to maximise the benefit and minimise the cost to us. In turn, this permits us to consider the unconscious mind as a very real and omnipresent driver of human behaviour.

2 More recently, psychologists and economists have taken the unconscious mind out of the narrow lens of the psychoanalytical school of thought and applied it more widely. System 1 and 2 thinking are examples of this. It provides researchers with a simple dualistic framework in which to understand thinking.

3 It seems we do not always have access to what sits behind decision-making post hoc. Studies into introspection make clear that in the absence of having access to the unconscious, we construct fiction to explain our behaviour. In market research, participants are no different and are prone to constructing narratives to explain behaviour that was largely a product of unconscious thinking. Consequently, when listening to stories participants tell, researchers should not take respondent commentary at face value without further probing.

4 We can address conscious thinking with direct questioning. To understand unconscious thinking, researchers need to frame questions in a way that allows respondents to access unconscious thinking. Laddering/means-end chain analysis and projective techniques are effective tools to elicit commentary that gets to the very heart of unconscious thinking.

3.1.6 References/further reading

Donald, I., and Canter, D. (1992). Intentionality and Fatality during the King's Cross Underground Fire. *European Journal of Social Psychology*, 22 (3), pp. 201–218.

Freud, S. (1915). The Unconscious. *S.E.*, 14, pp. 159–204.

Freud, S. (1923). The Ego and the Id. *S.E.*, 19, pp. 1–66.

Jung, C. G. (1933; reprint, 2001). *Modern Man in Search of His Soul*. London: Routledge Classics.

Jung, C. G. (1947). *On the Nature of the Psyche*. London: Ark Paperbacks.

Jung, C.G. (1971). *Psychological Types*. London: Routledge & Kegan Paul. Collected Works of C.G. Jung, Vol. 6.

Kahneman, D. (2011). *Thinking Fast and Slow*. London: Allen Lane.

Reynolds, T. J., and Gutman, J. (1988). Laddering Theory, Method, Analysis, and Interpretation. *Journal of Advertising Research*, 28 (1), pp. 11–31.
Wilson T. D., Lisle D. J., Schooler, J. W., Hodges, S.D., Klaaren, K.J., and LaFleur, S. J.
(1993). Introspecting About Reasons Can Reduce Post-choice Satisfaction. *Personality and Social Psychology Bulletin*, 19 (3), pp. 331–339.

3.1.6.1 *Want to know more?*

Most textbooks on personality theory or individual differences cover Freud and Jung. For a
more detailed review Freud and Jung's thinking the following texts are suggested.

Freud, S. (2010). *Collected Works: The Psychopathology of Everyday Life, The Theory of Sex-
uality, Beyond the Pleasure Principle, The Ego and the Id and The Future of an Illusion
Thinking*. Seattle: Pacific Publishing Studio.
Jung, C. G. (1964). *Man and His Symbols*. Sydney: Turtleback Books.

Regarding the adaptive unconscious, Timothy Wilson's book is the definitive text:
Wilson, T. (2002). *Strangers to Ourselves: Discovering the Adaptive Unconscious*. Cambridge,
MA: Harvard University Press.

3.2 Constructivism: understanding perceptions

3.2.1 *Defining constructivism*

Constructivists subscribe to a subjectivist research philosophy, believing that
we construe the world based on experience. In other words, the theory looks at
people's perceptions of the social world. The theory is an extension of symbolic
interactionism as discussed in Chapter 2. There is some debate about whether
there is one true reality or a myriad of constructed realities. Although what constructivists are clear on is through experience, our reality is created and knowledge is created therein. This is thought to be a continual process; with every new
social experience, our concept of reality is modified accordingly. A key exponent
of this approach is George Kelly. In this chapter, Kelly's personal construct theory
is reviewed along with the early work of Jean Piaget, which set the groundwork
for Kelly's deliberations. In the latter part of this chapter, we look at examples of
applying the principles of constructivism to behavioural research.

3.2.2 *Reviewing constructivism theory*

3.2.2.1 *Jean Piaget's genetic epistemology*

Piaget was a biologist by profession but is better known as a developmental psychologist. Piaget was concerned with the nature of thought and came up with
the theory of genetic epistemology, which refers to the study of the origins

and development of knowledge. Piaget observed that infants have certain basic sensory-motor skills that are used to explore their environment; as they gain more knowledge of the world, their ability to explore becomes even more sophisticated. In other words, Piaget's theory centres on knowledge structures that develop with experience (Piaget, 1936).

3.2.2.1.1 UNDERSTANDING THE PROCESS OF ASSIMILATION AND
    ACCOMMODATION

Knowledge structures are referred to as cognitive schemas (or scripts) that help us make sense of the world, they include actions, objects and concepts. Schemas are revised through experience by the cognitive process of adaption. Adaption involves assimilation and accommodation. When new information or experiences present themselves, we 'assimilate' knowledge into existing schemas or 'accommodate' by revising existing schemas or developing new schemas, as illustrated in Figure 3.8.

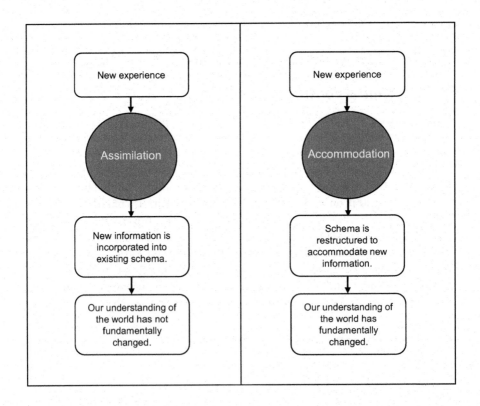

Figure 3.8 Assimilation and accommodation

3.2.2.1.2 MAINTAINING EQUILIBRIUM

It is thought that we can deal with most new information through the process of assimilation, although there will be occasions where assimilation will lead to contradictions or inconsistencies, resulting in disequilibrium. To address this, we accommodate and make changes to the existing schema or create a new schema to maintain equilibrium. Take the example of an experienced cyclist trying out a new bicycle. In this instance, the cyclist can assimilate the new bicycle experience into their existing schema for cycling. What if the same cyclist wants to ride a unicycle? In the absence of any experience of riding a unicycle, the cyclist will defer to the schema for riding a bicycle. However, the behavioural rules for riding a bicycle are different to that of a unicycle, and consequently, attempts at riding the unicycle are initially unsuccessful. This results in disequilibrium. As the cyclist practises on the unicycle, they learn new knowledge and restructure the schema to accommodate this new experience, resulting in equilibrium and hopefully a more competent unicyclist.

3.2.2.2 *George Kelly's personal construct theory*

Kelly developed a philosophy called constructive alternativism, where it is suggested that whilst there is one true reality, it is experienced from different perspectives or alternative constructions. Let us look at two different perspectives regarding the premium 4X4 car brand, Range Rover. Some might see Range Rovers as pretentious, road-hogging, environmentally damaging vehicles. Alternatively, others might identify strongly with the brand values of Range Rover, enjoy the elevated driving position and feel an increased sense of safety and security conferred to these types of vehicles. In this instance, we have one reality but two contrasting perspectives. Kelly built on this idea and developed personal construct theory (Kelly, 1955). The theory contends that people behave like scientists, formulating hypotheses, testing them and revising them accordingly. Through experience individuals 'construct' an understanding of the social world. In this theory, the unit of analysis is the construct, which has two core elements:

- Constructs represent the view individuals have constructed about the world as they experience it.
- Constructs indicate how individuals are likely to construe the world as they continue to experience it.

Kelly referred to constructs as 'personal' constructs because they are unique to the individual. Constructs are assumed to be bipolar, that is, existing within one of two states (or poles), such as tall versus short, high versus low, hot versus cold, active versus passive and so on.

With a focus on how the individual construes reality, Kelly's theory places emphasis on individual agency, rather than seeing the individual as a passive recipient of the environment they inhabit. Moreover, the theory suggests that differences in personality reflect differences in how individuals construe the world.

3.2.3 Measuring constructivism in behavioural research

3.2.3.1 The repertory grid interview

Kelly developed the role construct repertory test, which has come to be better known as the 'repertory grid'. It is not so much a test but more of an evaluation tool to identify and understand personal constructs. Let us look now at how to use repertory grids.

Each repertory grid is formed from a topic, elements, constructs and ratings:

- Topic: subject matter under inspection.
- Elements: can be different people, brands, products and so on. The elements can either be chosen by the participant or can be determined by the researcher.
- Constructs: this is where the elements are compared and contrasted with one another to produce several statements (or constructs) that help to define the topic matter. Each statement should be bipolar.
- Ratings: how we rate different elements on each construct, usually on a 1–5 response scale.

The process for conducting a repertory grid interview is outlined below using the example of chocolate brands:

1 Identify a topic (e.g. chocolate).
2 Select a set of elements (e.g. different chocolate brands, Guylian, Lindt, Green & Black's and Cadbury).
3 Take three of the elements and ask: "Can you tell me a way in which any two of these are different from the third?" (e.g. chocolate brand A is more bitter than brand B and C).
4 A qualifier ("In terms of…?") can be added to direct participants to consider the elements in a way appropriate to the purpose.
5 The above two-against-one question produces a bipolar construct (e.g. bitterness with the poles bitter and sweet).
6 Then turn the construct on a scale of 1 to 5 scale.
7 The participant then uses the scale to rate all the elements (e.g. participants will be asked to score each of the chocolate brands on the bitter to sweet scale).

The exercise is repeated until the participant is unable to come up with any more constructs.

The technique allows participants to talk about how they construe the world without any undue moderator bias. That is, the participant is entirely responsible for the creation of the personal constructs, not the moderator. Repertory grid interviews have been used in many different settings, including:

- Employee satisfaction, training and commitment.
- Organisational culture and identity.
- Brand analysis.
- Purchase behaviour.
- Proposition test and design.
- Counselling and therapeutic analysis.

This technique combines both qualitative and quantitative research in one tool. The development of the constructs provides rich qualitative insight and the ratings provide quantitative data which can be statistically analysed (which is particularly useful if there are many participants to process). On a cautionary note, the technique is relatively labour-intensive, both in terms of administration and analysis. As such, it will be important to ensure that sufficient time is factored into the research planning.

3.2.3.2 Self-characterisation technique and pre-tasks

In addition to the repertory grid interview, constructivists use self-characterisation as an investigative tool. Whilst the repertory grid interview involves both qualitative and quantitative analysis, the self-characterisation technique is exclusively qualitative. The technique is designed to tap into the participant's personal construct system, looking at their beliefs about themselves and consequently is sometimes referred to as the character sketch technique. The technique has its origins in the therapeutic environment but can be used in market research to help understand representations of self and others. For example, asking participants to create character sketches can help brands to 'get to know' specific groups/target segments. Prior to conducting a one-to-one interview, participants are asked to create a character sketch of themselves (as a pre-task), that is, a paragraph that explains how they see themselves. During the interview, the participant and moderator can discuss this in more detail. Further, the text can be analysed using textual analysis tools such as content and semiotic analysis (analysis techniques discussed in Section 2.5).

3.2.4 Constructivism theory in action

3.2.4.1 Assimilation and accommodation: 9/11 terrorist attacks

The media's response to Al-Qaeda's attack on American soil on 11 September 2001 could be considered a product of assimilation and accommodation. When the first plane hit the north tower of the World Trade Center, it was thought to be a tragic accident; at the time, news channels reported it as such. At this point, we are relying on assimilation, and there is no knowledge to suggest anything but a tragic accident. Not long after, the second plane hits the south tower, followed by a third plane hitting the west side of the Pentagon (the headquarters of the United States Department of Defence). This creates a disequilibrium and based on new information forces us to accommodate and acknowledge that this was not an accident but an act of terrorism. Now, we have an adapted schema that tells us that incidents involving planes hitting buildings are acts of terrorism.

3.2.4.2 Assimilation and accommodation: drug-taking amongst college students

As children, our parents might portray those that take drugs as undesirables, vagrants or even criminals to deter us from taking drugs. Consequently, we develop a negative schema about drug-taking. However, should we go to college or university, we will probably come across fellow students that use recreational drugs, but seem not to conform to our existing schema. This change in perspective results in a disequilibrium. To address this, we accommodate and revise our schema based on this new information. Now, we have a revised schema that not all people who take drugs are undesirables, vagrants or criminals.

3.2.4.3 Repertory grids: mobile phone networks

In this study, a mobile phone network provider was keen to understand how their brand was construed relative to the wider competitor set. Repertory grid interviews were used to identify how individuals distinguished one brand from another. Participants were given the following mobile network brands, Vodafone, EE, Giffgaff, O2, and Three and instructed to select groups of three and asked to state in what way were two of the brands different from the third. During this process, five constructs that distinguish different brands were identified. In Table 3.6, the grid used to score each brand by construct is presented.

In Figure 3.9, the mean score loadings for each brand are presented:

The outcomes of the research suggest that Vodafone and EE performed well in terms of network coverage but less so regarding value for money. Giffgaff and Three were seen as better value for money. Giffgaff is seen as a little different, more

Table 3.6 Constructs and elements/rating scale for UK mobile phone operators

Construct		Elements					
		Vodafone	EE	Giffgaff	O2	Three	
Value	Good value						Expensive
Coverage	Good coverage						Poor coverage
Personality	Egalitarian						Conservative
Warmth	Warm						Cold
Innovation	Innovators						Followers

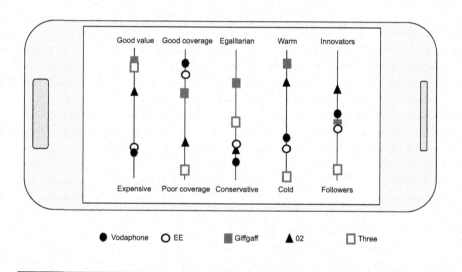

Figure 3.9 Repertory grid outcomes – mobile network brand example

egalitarian than other brands. Except for O2, most brands did not perform well in regard to innovation.

3.2.4.4 Repertory grids: washing machine brand review

In this study, a washing machine manufacturer wanted to understand what value judgements consumers make about different washing machine brands. Repertory grid interviews were used to tease out different constructs which were seen to define consumer choice. Participants were given the following washing machine

Table 3.7 Constructs and elements/rating scale for washing machine brands

Construct		Elements						
		Miele	*Bosch*	*Hotpoint*	*LG*	*Electrolux*	*Beko*	
Value	Good value							Expensive
Reliability	Reliable							Unreliable
Simplicity	Simple to use							Difficult to use
Running cost	Low							High
Cycle	Short cycle							Long cycle
Maintenance	Easy							Difficult
Innovation	Innovators							Followers

manufacturer brands, Miele, Bosch, Hotpoint, LG, Electrolux and Beko and instructed to select groups of three and state in what way were two of the brands different from the third. Seven constructs that helped to distinguish brands were identified. In Table 3.7, the grid used to score each brand by construct is presented.

The outcomes of the repertory grid task can be analysed quantitatively by using multidimensional scaling (a statistical technique used to help visualise the difference and similarities of variables). In so doing, we can use the data from the repertory grids to build a market map, as illustrated in Figure 3.10.

In interpreting the market map, brands that are nearest to each other have most in common, and brands that are furthest apart have the least in common. Using the same principle, the position of the poles of any given construct helps

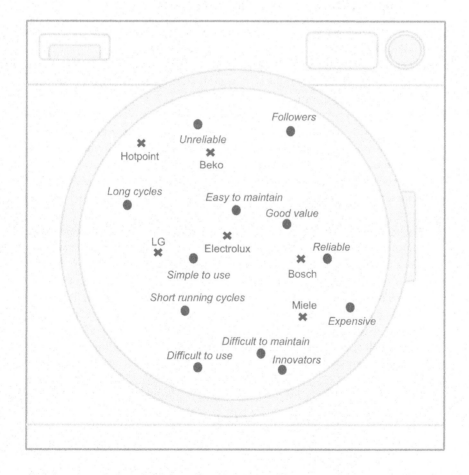

Figure 3.10 Repertory Grid outcomes – washing machine brand example

to define each brand. Different constellations of brands and construct poles help to define brand territories. The results suggest that consumers saw Hotpoint and Beko as unreliable with long running cycles. In contrast, Bosch and Miele were thought to be reliable albeit expensive. Electrolux and LG sat in the middle ground and were thought to be simple to use and of good value.

Whilst repertory grid interviews are rich in content, they can be time-consuming to administer. In a group or one-to-one setting, it will be important to ensure there is sufficient time to conduct the exercise. That said, with patience, the repertory grid interview is a powerful tool to understand the world through the lens of the participant.

3.2.5 Implications for behavioural research

1 Constructivists argue that differences in personality reflect how we construe the social world.
2 Schemas are cognitive scripts that help us make sense of the social world. Through a process of adaption, we assimilate and accommodate knowledge to maintain equilibrium.
3 The repertory grid interview is a useful tool in teasing out constructs that sit behind product choice and brand advocacy. The technique lends itself well to subject matter where participants might struggle to articulate how they feel about something using standard interviewing techniques.
4 The repertory grid provides a framework in which to guide not only the participant but the moderator. Further, participants can talk about how they construe the world without any undue moderator bias.
5 The data accrued from the repertory grid is rich in detail and with careful analysis can be immensely valuable in unpacking core drivers of behaviour.
6 On a cautionary note, the technique is relatively labour-intensive, both in terms of administration and analysis. In choosing this approach, consideration will need to be given in terms of time and possible cost implications.
7 Self-characterisation is a useful technique to connect with participants' personal construct systems, allowing the researcher to understand representations of self and others. This technique can be used in marketing to locate and profile a target audience.

3.2.6 References/further reading

Kelly, G. (1955). *The Repertory Test. The Psychology of Personal Constructs 1. A Theory of Personality*. New York: W.W Norton.
Piaget, J., and Cook, M. T. (1936; reprint, 1992). *The Origins of Intelligence in Children*. New York: International University Press.

3.2.6.1 *Want to know more?*

As with other personality theories, there are many textbooks on personality and individual differences which detail Kelly's work. Alternatively, you can go back to the original source text, as detailed above.

3.3 Personality traits: measuring temperament

3.3.1 *Defining personality traits*

Should we attempt to describe a friend or colleague's personality, we might use adjectives like kind, generous, intelligent but fail to elaborate much beyond this. In the past, psychologists sought to describe personality based on a set of predetermined personality types. Yet we are so different that it can be difficult to categorise people in this way. Given this, some psychologists use temperament and traits as a proxy for personality. A trait tells us something of the character of a personality without trying to explain personality *in toto*. Traits reflect our thoughts, feelings and behaviours and define how we respond to things in the world we inhabit. It is thought that traits are biologically determined and, therefore, are relatively stable over time. Of course, the process of socialisation will have some impact on our temperament, so it would be wrong to assume that traits can be explained solely by biology.

3.3.2 *Reviewing personality trait theory*

3.3.2.1 *Gordon Allport's trait theory*

The American psychologist Allport was one of the founders of personality psychology and put forward one of the earliest models of trait theory. Allport observed that there were over 4,000 different words to describe personality in the English language dictionary (Allport, 1937). Allport organised these words into cardinal, central and secondary trait levels, as illustrated in Table 3.8.

3.3.2.2 *Raymond Cattell's 16-personality traits*

The psychologist Cattell took Allport's 4,000 traits, removed uncommon traits and combined similar traits to get down to 171 traits. Cattell then used factor analysis (a technique that identifies overarching factors or dimensions from a dataset) to reduce this down to 16 personality traits (Cattell, 1957). From this, Cattell developed the 16-personality factors questionnaire. The questionnaire is used in therapeutic settings to this day. Despite reducing Allport's traits down to 16, Cattell's traits have been criticised for being too broad.

Table 3.8 Trait levels

Trait levels	Definition
Cardinal traits	Are rare and dominant: • Few people have a single dominant trait that explains their personality. • These traits often emerge later in life and become synonymous with personality. • Examples might include general terms such as Don Juan, Christ-like, Machiavellian and narcissistic.
Central traits	Are more common and less dominant: • These traits are the foundations of personality and shape behaviour. • Examples include friendliness, honesty, intelligence and shyness.
Secondary traits	Are circumstantial, appearing in certain situations: • Secondary traits are important in demonstrating the complexity of personality. • Examples might include being impatient when waiting in line or being anxious about public speaking.

3.3.2.3 Hans Eysenck's temperament dimensions

As discussed earlier in this chapter, Jung was one of the first to popularise the notion of extroversion and introversion (Jung, 1921). Whilst our understanding of extroversion and introversion has evolved from the original premise of opposing attitudes, Jung's theorising set the foundations for the development of contemporary trait theories of personality, in particular, the work of Eysenck.

Eysenck is arguably one of the most influential figures in the field of trait theory. Eysenck was a research psychologist who dedicated his life to the study of personality and was a prodigious writer, leaving a significant body of work behind. Eysenck's standpoint was that personality is preordained, that is, a product of physiology and genetics (Eysenck, 1952, 1967). Eysenck applied experimental design and used multivariate statistics to identify temperament dimensions (like Cattell, Eysenck used factor analysis, a technique that identifies overarching factors or dimensions from a dataset). Eysenck's emphasis on experimental design and statistical analysis placed him firmly in the objectivism research philosophy. In his original work, Eysenck suggested two broad dimensions, neuroticism-emotional stability and extroversion-introversion, let us look at each in turn.

3.3.2.3.1 NEUROTICISM-EMOTIONAL STABILITY DIMENSION

Neurotic behaviour is characterised by overreacting to a situation, exhibiting a tendency to worry or stress unduly; the opposite end of the spectrum is emotional stability, as illustrated in Figure 3.11.

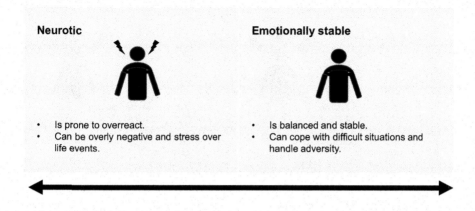

Neurotic

- Is prone to overreact.
- Can be overly negative and stress over life events.

Emotionally stable

- Is balanced and stable.
- Can cope with difficult situations and handle adversity.

Figure 3.11 Neuroticism-emotional stability dimension

Eysenck believed that where an individual sits on the neuroticism-emotional stability dimension can largely be accounted for by the sympathetic nervous system (part of the autonomic nervous system) that is responsible for our reactions to emergencies. In a 'fight or flight' response, our brain sends signals to the adrenal glands to release the neurotransmitters noradrenaline and adrenaline, that prime our muscles for action. It is thought that some people have more sensitive sympathetic nervous systems than others and consequently are prone to neurotic behaviour. Whilst this might seem rather deterministic, psychologists do believe that we have a genetic predisposition to neuroticism.

3.3.2.3.2 EXTROVERSION-INTROVERSION DIMENSION

In addition to the neuroticism-emotional stability, Eysenck suggested the extroversion-introversion dimension, as illustrated in Figure 3.12.

Like the neuroticism-emotional stability dimension, what distinguishes an extrovert from an introvert is how they respond to stimuli. As a rule of thumb, extroverts crave high-stimulation environments; introverts are at their best in low-stimulation environments. Again, Eysenck argued that where we sit on the extroversion-introversion dimension is accounted for by biology, where extroverts have a slightly lower state of arousal than introverts and consequently require greater stimulation.

3.3.2.3.3 AMBIVERTS: THE FORGOTTEN MIDDLE GROUND

It is important to note that the extroversion-introversion dimension is not a dichotomy but a continuum, where people can load somewhere on the dimension. For example, you might not identify as either an introvert or an extrovert,

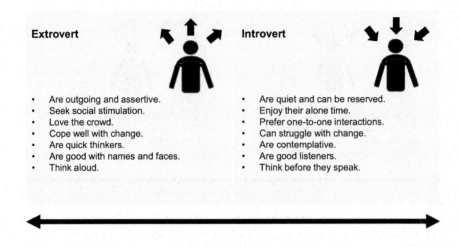

Figure 3.12 Extroversion-introversion dimension

but an ambivert, where you sit somewhere between the two traits. You might be quiet and contemplative, but nonetheless be very sociable. You might enjoy the throng of the party or a crowd, but after a time need some quiet time to recharge. You might be relatively open and gregarious with close friends but more reserved with people you are not so familiar with. In these instances, the chances are you are an ambivert. Ambiverts are adaptable and able to play to their strengths by calling upon extroversion or introversion traits depending on the situation.

3.3.2.3.4 EXTROVERT CULTURAL BIAS

There is a cultural bias towards extroverts, who are often seen as somehow better than introverts. This view has come to be challenged. For example, Susan Cain, in her book, *Quiet: The Power of Introverts in a World That Can't Stop Talking* (2002) argued that western societies favour action over quiet contemplation, which plays to the strengths of the extrovert. It does seem that we admire (even revere) extroverts at the expense of introverts. This bias is present in most walks of life. Take the work setting, often we favour those that are charismatic or gregarious, who are comfortable giving a presentation to the company or running a brainstorming session. In marketing, outgoing and opinionated personality traits are used to sell products, where a link is made between the product and the extrovert's 'dynamic and engaging' lifestyle. Intriguingly, there is little thought on how to harness the power of the introvert to sell the message. Typically, extroverts are considered better leaders. In practice, individuals play to their strengths and weaknesses at the moment. Extroverts lead from the front, relying on personality to persuade others to follow their vision and can make quick decisions. In contrast, introverts will let others shine, drawing on the qualities of others and will listen and respond to the feedback of others.

3.3.2.3.5 INTROVERSION AND SHYNESS

There is a misconception that introverts are shy. This is not necessarily the case; Cain argues that shyness is about a fear of social judgement and humiliation. Introverts are quiet and contemplative and enjoy alone time to recharge, which is different from being shy.

3.3.2.3.6 PSYCHOTICISM-NORMALITY DIMENSION

Eysenck later added a third dimension, psychoticism-normality (Eysenck and Eysenck, 1976). According to Eysenck, psychoticism includes traits such as aggressiveness, manipulation, tough-mindedness, risk-taking, irresponsibility and impulsivity. Normality is essentially the opposite of these traits. Eysenck thought that psychoticism was a product of high levels of testosterone.

Although psychoticism is mostly associated with criminal behaviour and mental illness, there is much debate about a link between psychoticism and creativity. This notion plays to a commonly held belief that the price of creativity is madness (best personified by Vincent van Gogh cutting off his ear in a fit of mania after an argument with a fellow artist, Paul Gauguin, the artist with whom he had been working with in Arles, southern France). In reality, the academic evidence is inconclusive, though there is evidence to suggest that less severe forms of psychoticism are linked to creativity (e.g. Claridge and Blakey, 2009; Nelson and Rawlings, 2010).

3.3.2.4 The big five personality trait theory

It has been argued that Eysenck's three dimensions are overly simplistic, whilst Cattell's 16 traits are overly complicated. Based on nearly a century of research, there is now a consensus amongst the psychological community that there are broadly five dimensions. The net result is the big five personality trait theory. The five dimensions are commonly referred to by the acronym OCEAN and are presented in Table 3.9.

The big five personality trait theory is a synthesis of different strands of empirical evidence to form a single unifying model of personality traits. Research

Table 3.9 Big five personality traits

Dimension	Loading	
	High	*Low*
Openness	Curious, open to new ideas, artistic and creative, but can lead to unpredictable and high-risk behaviour.	Down to earth, practical, and conventional.
Conscientiousness	Dutiful, orderly, thorough and competent.	Impulsive, careless and disorganised.
Extroversion	Sociable, impulsive, cheerful, talkative and spontaneous.	Quiet, contemplative and values alone time.
Agreeableness	Interested and cares for others, altruistic and warm.	Not interested in others, suspicious and critical.
Neuroticism	Anxious and involved, self-conscious and emotional.	Calm, relaxed and stable.

evidence supports the notion that there are a set of broad personality traits that are germane to humans, irrespective of culture or creed. However, researchers should be mindful that not all these traits are in evidence at the same time. Personality is complex and multifaceted, where an individual might display certain traits but not others, in different situations.

3.3.2.5 Dark trait dimensions

Whilst the big five personality trait theory is considered a good overall measure of personality traits, academics have suggested that there might be a set of additional darker more malevolent traits, namely: narcissism, psychopathy and Machiavellianism. These traits have come to be known as the dark triad. There is some overlap between dark traits, with a lack of empathy for others, common to all. In Table 3.10, all three dimensions are presented.

Table 3.10 Dark trait dimensions

Dimension	Loading	
	High	*Low*
Narcissism	Vanity, superiority and lack of empathy.	Empathetic and limited focus on self.
Psychopathy	Antisocial, impulsive and unemotional.	Remorseful, social and considered.
Machiavellianism	Manipulative, exploitative, self-interested and amoral.	Moral, conscientious and agreeable.

Given the nature of dark trait dimensions, it is of no surprise that these traits have been used to predict a vast array of socially aversive behaviour, including:

■ Aggression and violence.
■ Self-enhancement and achievement.
■ Infidelity and sexual behaviour.
■ Coercive work behaviours.
■ Gambling addiction.
■ Online trolling.

The American serial killer Ted Bundy is often associated with dark traits. Whilst his demeanour was both charming and affable, he was manipulative and cunning using others to get what he wanted. Further, Bundy exhibited calculated predatory aggression and enjoyed playing to an audience. In market research, we do not expect (or want) to find the next Bundy, but it follows that like the light dimensions of the big five personality trait theory, participants will load somewhere on the darker dimensions.

There is evidence to suggest that in recent times, society has become more narcissistic. The author, Bill Bryson travelled across Britain, initially for his book *Notes from a Small Island* (1995) and latterly for his follow-up book *The Road to Little Dribbling, More Notes from a Small Island* (2015). Bryson observed that whilst living standards were much improved in Britain, the British had become greedier and more selfish. Similar observations were made by Will Storr, in his book *Selfie Book How the West Became Self-obsessed* (2018). Storr explored how our sense of self has evolved over the years, from ancient Greece to the humanistic movement in California in the 1960s, right up to the present day. Storr argued that we have become social perfectionists, with an ever-greater sense of our self and our abilities. Storr concluded that parental overpraising and the internet, amongst other things, has led to the emergence of a generation of narcissists. If we take the internet as a case in point, social networking sites present the narcissist with an ideal playground, in which to upload selfies and make commentary about their everyday lives in promoting an inflated sense of self-worth. The emergence of intellectual egalitarianism might also have a part to play, where we are dissuaded from intelligent debate because it is deemed undemocratically elitist, and the views of the uninitiated, no matter how weird and wonderful, demand to be given equal weight of importance to that of academics, doctors and politicians.

3.3.3 *Measuring personality traits in behavioural research*

3.3.3.1 *Neuroticism-emotional stability and extroversion-introversion dimensions*

3.3.3.1.1 QUANTITATIVE MEASUREMENT

Eysenck personality questionnaire (EPQ) measures both neuroticism-emotional stability and introversion-extroversion dimensions (Eysenck and Eysenck, 1975). The questionnaire contains 90 items and takes 20 minutes to complete. The EPS-S is a short-form version, that consists of 48 items and takes 10 minutes to complete (Eysenck et al., 1985).

3.3.3.1.2 QUALITATIVE IMMERSION

In a qualitative setting, questions should centre on the following key themes:

- Sociability.
- Impulsiveness.
- Quietness.
- Thoughtfulness.
- Spontaneity.
- Outgoingness.

In addition to the above, looking at how participants recharge will be important. Generally, an extrovert will do so by socialising, whilst an introvert might prefer some quiet time. In direct conversation, some of the above themes might be difficult to address. Presenting participants with a scenario and asking them how they imagine they would behave can help elicit a response.

3.3.3.2 Big five personality traits

The NEO personality inventory is designed to measure openness, conscientiousness, extroversion, agreeableness and neuroticism dimensions (Costa and McCrae, 1985, 1992). The inventory has been continually improved, with updates to reflect changes in norms over time. The NEO PI-3 is considered the gold standard of trait measurement, although it consists of 240 questions and takes up to 40 minutes to complete. In response to this, Costa and McCrae developed a short-form version that consists of 60 items (NEO-FFI-R). In market research, even the short-form questionnaire with 60 questions might be tricky to administer, particularly when questions about profile and personality must be balanced against the need for core research questions. In commercial research, this might necessitate a more pragmatic approach, where not all items are asked, but key trait questions are selected to gain an indicative view of temperament.

3.3.3.3 Dark traits

3.3.3.3.1 QUANTITATIVE MEASUREMENT

Responding to an increased interest in the dark traits, the psychologists, Peter Jonason and Gregory Webster (2010) developed a 12-item question battery, inventively called the 'dirty dozen'.

3.3.3.3.2 QUALITATIVE IMMERSION

It will be challenging to directly discuss dark traits with participants in any detail. Looking out for tendencies that suggest a dark trait, in general conversation, is a practical alternative. In Table 3.11, key darker traits to look out for are presented.

3.3.4 Personality trait theory in action

3.3.4.1 Extroversion-introversion: advertising response

Chang (2001) was concerned with whether identifying as an introvert or extrovert would influence how individuals view advertising campaigns. It was hypothesised that introverts and extroverts will evaluate products differently irrespective of the

Table 3.11 Question areas for measuring dark traits

Dark traits	Definition
Machiavellianism	• Truthfulness, manipulation and duplicity.
Psychopathy	• Remorsefulness, insensitivity, morality and cynicism.
Narcissism	• Need for admiration, desire for attention, need for status and prestige and extent of favour-seeking.

advertising employed. This was based on the premise that introverts are motivated to avoid costs, whereas extroverts are motivated by rewards. In this study, the test product was a bottle of water (which was found to be a low-involving product in a pre-test; a high-involving product might result in different responses based on whether the participants identified as an introvert or extrovert). Marketing messages and product imagery was created by the advertising agency, Ogilvy. A total of 396 participants took part in the study. Participants were asked to express their views about the messages and product imagery. It was found that irrespective of the message, those that identified as extroverts looked at the messaging more positively, with introverts responding more negatively. Chang was also interested in the possible impact of the discrepancy between how participants perceived themselves and the product image portrayed in marketing campaigns. As expected, the greater the discrepancy between participant self and the product image portrayed in the advertising, the more likely it was that the advertising campaign was seen negatively. This study demonstrates the importance of playing to not only the extrovert but the introvert when considering campaign effectiveness.

3.3.4.2 Extroversion-introversion: small business loans

In this study, research was commissioned to explore how banks can use digital enhancements to improve the loan application process for small businesses. It was suggested that where businesses sat on the extroversion-introversion dimension would impact on how they go about applying for small business loans. It was

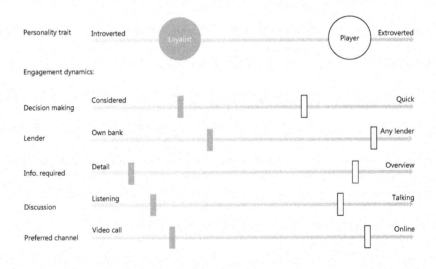

Figure 3.13 Extroversion-introversion small business groups

hypothesised that more extroverted businesses would require less support and be comfortable applying online, whilst those who were more introverted would want more support and favour a video call. Largely, this hypothesis was borne out. A total of 30 qualitative interviews were conducted amongst small businesses. The results of the study are presented in Figure 3.13.

Two groups emerged, loyalists and players, that identified strongly with introversion and extroversion, respectively.

- The players, were happy to consider any lender, required only a brief overview of the loan product, were keen to express their views and favoured an online application.
- The loyalists, considered their main bank as the first port of call for a loan, required a more detailed explanation of the loan product, were keen to listen and favoured a video call.

3.3.4.3 *Dark traits: the rise of the internet troll*

Online trolling is where individuals are subjected to rude and unpleasant commentary that has little purpose beyond upsetting the recipient. Internet trolls will post inflammatory commentary, lie and cajole to elicit a response. Interestingly, when internet trolls are tested on the dark dimensions, they load much higher than those that do not engage in such activity (Lopes and Yu, 2017). Social media platforms have been slow to address the problem of internet trolling, clearly more needs to be done to protect users from this type of behaviour, whilst balancing the need for self-expression.

3.3.4.4 *Dark traits: workplace behaviour*

Researchers have looked at the relationship between undesirable workplace behaviour and dark traits. Typically, there is a correlation between dark traits and negative workplace behaviours, including:

- Unethical behaviour.
- Poor job performance.
- White-collar crime.
- Negative perceptions by other staff.

Dark trait behaviour can result in greater achievement, although often at the detriment of others. For instance, in Oliver James's book *Office Politics: How to Thrive in a World of Lying, Backstabbing and Dirty Tricks* (2013), it was suggested that success in the workplace is dependent on office politics. It seems success demands a degree of 'hustling' where blame is assigned and credit for work appropriated. The best hustlers are those that exhibit dark traits, progressing by making a virtue of bullying and manipulation.

3.3.5 Implications for behavioural research

1 Trait theorists contend that differences in personality reflect where individuals load on different temperament dimensions.

2 The extent to which traits are hardwired into the sympathetic nervous system is debatable, although it seems we are born with a predisposition to behave in a certain way and through socialisation, our temperament is determined.

3 A trait is not a personality type, but a measure of thoughts, feelings and behaviour. Testing for different traits provides useful profiling information. For instance, when looking to launch a new brand, knowing about personality traits that best align with that brand will help inform the marketing brief and subsequent advertising plan.

4 In interpreting research results, researchers need to guard against cultural bias towards extroverts to the detriment of introverts. Further, researchers should not forget that many participants will end up somewhere in the middle, neither an extrovert nor introvert, but an ambivert.

5 The big five personality trait theory provides researchers with an overall robust measure of personality traits. That said, even the short-form of the inventory takes time to complete. In market research, we need to balance the core research questions with those that address profile and personality. This often necessitates a more pragmatic approach, where based on the research problem, key traits are selected to gain an indicative view of temperament. For example, the extroversion-introversion dimension is one of the more important dimensions when looking at advertising response.

6 It is reasonable to assume that to a greater or lesser extent, participants will exhibit both light and dark traits. Focusing exclusively on light traits will preclude researchers from seeing the full nature of temperament as a determinant of behaviour.

7 Given personality traits are relatively stable over time, researchers can make predictions about human behaviour with confidence.

3.3.6 References/further reading

Allport, G. W. (1937). *Personality: A Psychological Interpretation*. New York: Holt, Rinehart & Winston.

Bryson, B. (1995). *Notes from a Small Island*. London: Penguin Random House.

Bryson, B. (2015). *The Road to Little Dribbling, More Notes from a Small Island.* London: Penguin Random House.

Cain, S. (2002). *Quiet: The Power of Introverts in a World That Can't Stop Talking.* New York: Penguin.

Cattell, R. B. (1957). *Personality and Motivation Structure and Measurement.* New York: World Book.

Chang, C. (2001). The Impacts of Personality Differences on Product Evaluations. In M. C. Gilly, and J. Meyers-Levy, Ga, V. (Eds.), *NA – Advances in Consumer Research,* 28. Association for Consumer Research, pp. 26–33.

Claridge, G., and Blakey, S. (2009). Schizotypy and Affective Temperament: Relationships with Divergent Thinking and Creativity Styles. *Personality and Individual Differences,* 46 (8), pp. 820–826.

Costa, P. T., and McCrae, R. R. (1985). *The NEO Personality Inventory Manual.* Odessa, FL: Psychological Assessment Resources.

Costa, P. T., and McCrae, R. R. (1992). *Revised NEO Personality Inventory (NEO-PI-R) and NEO Five-Factor Inventory (NEO-FFI) Professional Manual.* Odessa, FL: Psychological Assessment Resources.

Eysenck, H. J. (1952). *The Scientific Study of Personality.* London: Routledge & Kegan Paul PLC.

Eysenck, H. J. (1967). *The Biological Basis of Personality* (Vol. 689). Springfield, IL: Thomas.

Eysenck, H. J., and Eysenck, S. B. G. (1975). *Manual of the Eysenck Personality Questionnaire.* London: Hodder and Stoughton.

Eysenck, H. J., and Eysenck, S. B. G. (1976). *Eysenck Personality Questionnaire. Educational and Industrial Testing Service.* London: Hodder and Stoughton.

Eysenck, S. B. G., Eysenck, H. J., and Barrett, P. (1985). A Revised Version of the Psychoticism Scale. *Personality and Individual Differences,* 6 (1), pp. 21–29.

Jonason, P. K., and Webster, G. D. (2010). The Dirty Dozen: A Concise Measure of the Dark Triad. *Psychological Assessment,* 22 (2), pp. 420–432.

Jung, C. G. (1921). *Psychological Type.* Zurich: Rascher.

Lopes, B., and Yu, H. (2017). Who Do You Troll and Why: An Investigation into the Relationship Between the Dark Triad Personalities and Online Trolling Behaviours Towards Popular and Less Popular Facebook Profiles. *Computers in Human Behavior,* 77, pp. 69–76.

Nelson, B., and Rawlings, D. (2010). Relating Schizotypy and Personality to the Phenomenology of Creativity. *Schizophrenia Bulletin,* 36, pp. 388–399.

Oliver, J. (2013). *Office Politics: How to Thrive in a World of Lying, Backstabbing and Dirty Tricks.* London: Vermilion.

Storr, W. (2018). *Selfie: How the West Became Self-Obsessed.* London: Picador.

3.3.6.1 Want to know more?

Most textbooks on personality theory or individual differences will review the key protagonists in this field of psychology. For a more detailed view of trait theory, the following book provides a good overview and looks at traits in different situations, along with trait stability over time:

Mathews, G., Deary, I. J., and Whiteman, M. C. (2009). *Personality Traits.* New York: Cambridge University Press.

Regarding dark personality traits, the following journal article provides a good overview:
Paulhus, D. L. (2014). Toward a Taxonomy of Dark Personalities. *Current Directions in Psychological Science*, 23, pp. 421–426.

3.4 Conditioning: responding to environmental stimuli

3.4.1 Defining conditioned behaviour

Conditioning is a behaviourist approach to explaining human behaviour. Behaviourism is concerned with objectively observing the relationship between environmental stimulus and response. In other words, behaviourists focus on cause and effect. This rather deterministic approach to human behaviour places behaviourism in the objectivist research philosophy. Within the behaviourist's doctrine, the theory of conditioning contends that a reaction or response to an object or stimulus can be modified by learning or conditioning. Learning involves both strengthening and weakening of an association between a stimulus and response. Behaviourists argue that personality develops and changes through a series of learned experiences. Many behaviours are self-evident because we associate either a positive or negative outcome with those behaviours. For instance, we tend to reframe from talking over someone, because we have learnt that this is considered to be impolite. We associate the smell of certain foods with nausea because in the past they have made us sick. Reaching for our mobile phone, when we hear a chime or when the phone vibrates, is also conditioned behaviour, where we have learnt to associate chimes and vibrations with the arrival of new messages. Below we look at classical and operant conditioning, before reviewing contemporary behaviourist theory.

3.4.2 Reviewing conditioning theory

3.4.2.1 Ivan Pavlov's classical conditioning

Conditioning can be traced back to the early work of the psychologist, Pavlov, who observed that dogs salivate in response to food (Pavlov, 1902). Pavlov noted that dogs salivated not only in the presence of food but also when stimulus associated with food was present. Exploring this observation in an experimental environment, Pavlov presented a stimulus (a clicking metronome) before food was given to dogs. After a few repeats – when the metronome was presented in isolation of the food – it elicited salivation, whereby, the dog had learnt an association between the metronome and food. Given the response is learned by association,

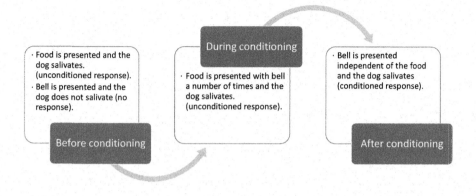

Figure 3.14 Key stages in conditioning

it is considered a conditioned response. The conditioned response worked with a variety of stimuli, including a whistle, tuning fork and a bell. The key stages of classical conditioning are presented in Figure 3.14.

Although Pavlov's work was groundbreaking in its day, arguably human behaviour is infinitely more complex than that of dogs. To address this, Skinner's influential work on operant conditioning is discussed below.

3.4.2.2 Burrhus Frederick Skinner's operant conditioning

Skinner felt that classical conditioning was an overly simplistic explanation of behaviour, where conditioning assumes that behaviour is largely involuntary. Skinner claimed that behaviour is voluntary, believing the best way to understand behaviour was to look at the consequences of behaviour. The central tenet of his theory is that we 'operate' in our environment, rather than passively respond to it. During operating we come across positive or negative reinforcement and positive or negative punishment stimulus that helps to increase or decrease the incident of a behaviour 'the operant' (Skinner, 1938). Naturally, we might come across neutral stimulus which will have no impact on behaviour whatsoever, as illustrated in Figure 3.15.

3.4.2.2.1 POSITIVE REINFORCEMENT AND PUNISHMENT

In positive reinforcement and punishment, a *stimulus is added*. For example, a positive reinforcement might be your line manager giving you a pay rise in recognition of your work, which motivates you to work harder for further reward.

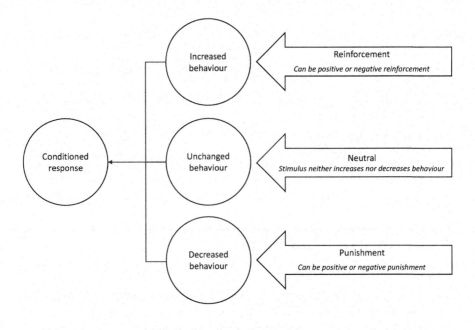

Figure 3.15 Reinforcement, neutral and punishment conditioned responses

A positive punishment might be your line manager giving you a warning because of your behaviour, which deters you from continuing with that behaviour.

3.4.2.2.2 NEGATIVE REINFORCEMENT AND PUNISHMENT

In negative reinforcement and punishment, the *stimulus is removed*. For example, a negative reinforcement might be your line manager no longer criticising your work, which motivates you to work harder to avoid the prospect of further criticism. A negative punishment might be your line manager usually praises good work but stops providing feedback, which makes you less inclined to do good work.

The power of reinforcement and punishment is related to the immediacy, consistency, size and, finally, frequency of the stimulus.

3.4.2.3 Little Albert experiment

Both classical and operant conditioning allude to generalisations; with a conditioned response, there can be a tendency to generalise from the conditioned stimulus to another similar stimulus. One of the more infamous examples of stimulus generalisation is Watson and Raynor's (1920) little Albert experiment. In the

Table 3.12 Basic behavioural repertoires

Basic behavioural repertoires	Definition
Sensory-motor repertoire	• Sensory-motor skills, attention and social skills.
Language-cognitive repertoire	• Receptive language and expressive language.
Emotional-motivational repertoire	• Positive and negative patterns of emotional reactions that direct behaviour.

experiment, Albert, a nine-month-old child, showed no fear of white rats, but when a white rat was paired with loud scary sounds the child began to cry. Over time, the boy began to be fearful of objects that were similar in appearance to the white rat. In so doing, the child generalised from the rat to other white objects. Although ethically questionable, the experiment does demonstrate the power of conditioned behaviour and generalisations.

3.4.2.4 Arthur Staat's psychological behaviourism

As noted earlier, behaviourists argue that personality develops and changes through learned experiences. With an emphasis on what can be observed, there is little acknowledgement of personality as an internal construct. However, behaviourism has evolved into a theory that is built on the foundations of Watson and Skinner's theorising but is less deterministic. An example of this is psychological behaviourism (Staat, 1996). Previously, behaviourism research was based solely on animals. The psychologist, Staat was one of the first behaviourists to study human behaviour and formulated the theory of psychological behaviourism. The theory contends that personality is a product of learned behaviour through the interplay of environmental stimulus, biology and psychological factors. According to Staat, we learn new behaviour within the context of previously learned basic behavioural repertoires (BBRs). There are three BBRs, as illustrated in Table 3.12.

As a child we have little experience of the world, with time, we learn BBRs which guide behaviour in specific situations. As such, how we experience the world depends on our BBRs. It is thought that learned BBRs help shape our personality and as BBRs are modified through experience, personality is constituted. It follows that by observing BBRs, we can observe personality. Biology is also an important mediating factor, providing the mechanisms for learning and performing.

3.4.3 Measuring conditioning in behavioural research

In market research, it will not be uncommon for behaviour to be attributable to some form of conditioning. Researchers also witness examples of generalisations in behaviour, that can result in socially unacceptable behaviour or poor decision-making. Below, is a list of question areas that have proven effective in understanding conditioning, both in terms of type and consequences:

- What are the circumstances in which conditioned behaviour change occurs?
- How important is positive versus negative conditioning?
- How do research participants use stimulus that is available to them to make decisions?
- What value do research participants place on different forms of stimulus?
- To what extent is behaviour generalised and under what circumstances?
- How cognisant are participants about the conditioned decisions they make?

3.4.4 Conditioning theory in action

The principles of conditioning continue to be influential in the application of behavioural therapy but also amongst psychologists, marketeers and economists. Detailed below are some examples of these applications.

3.4.4.1 Encouraging healthy food choices

The American supermarket Lowe's Pay & Save placed large green plastic arrows on the floor of their supermarkets to direct customers to the healthy vegetables. Even though the arrows directed customers to the left (where typically customers turn to the right), most customers turned left. In another example, a mirror was placed in the supermarket trollies. The purpose of the mirror was to get customers to look at themselves and then reflect upon their grocery purchase decisions. In both instances, vegetable purchasing increased significantly (*The New York Times*, 28 August 2013). Interestingly, rather than communicating the consequences of a poor diet or taxing high sugar products, these simple persuasion techniques positively reinforced healthy food purchases.

3.4.4.2 Helping people to give up smoking

Positive reinforcement has been used to encourage people to give up smoking. During a six-month period, people were given a savings account with money deposited in it and told if they gave up smoking, they would get to keep the money in the account, otherwise the money would be donated to charity (Giné et al., 2010). At the end of the six months, a urine test was administered to ascertain if the participants had given up smoking or not. Although the money was a sufficient incentive to give up when the incentive was withdrawn many returned to smoking. This would suggest that the reinforcement needs to be longer term to ensure sustained behavioural change.

3.4.4.3 Conditioning through product endorsement

Many brands use conditioning to associate their products with an action or emotion that helps promote them. For instance, linking professional sports stars to sports brands can create a powerful positive association. Intriguingly, the association does not have to be logical, for instance, an athlete can be associated with a non-sport brand where the link between the brand and the athlete is at best, tenuous. For example, in the Müller Light adverts an association is made with Katerina Johnson Thompson's heptathlon success and the brand's low-fat products, and similarly, the Virgin Media adverts made an association between the sprinter Usain Bolt's success and faster broadband.

3.4.4.4 Consumer demand and reinforcement

Economists and psychologists have sought to understand consumer demand as a measure of consumption. Research has looked at different commodities and price elasticity. Certain commodities are more elastic than others; for instance, consumers tend to be more sensitive to price rises on household groceries but less so on fuel. In such instances, the relative value of the commodity is the reinforcement. For instance, the most expensive item on a restaurant menu is unlikely to be purchased by many; however, it serves to make the second most expensive item on the menu seem good value. Unbeknownst to the diners, behaviour is being conditioned, as the most expensive item acts as a decoy.

3.4.5 Implications for behavioural research

1 Whilst humans are infinitely more complex than Pavlov's dogs, they still exhibit conditioned behaviour. Conditioning is an important driver of human behaviour, both in terms of reinforcement and punishment. As researchers, we need to be mindful that the reason behind a behaviour can be as simple as a response to stimuli.

2 It seems that in many instances we are not aware that we are responding to conditioning, suggesting that conditioned behaviour is instinctive. As such, researchers need to be cautious and not take participant commentary about why they behaved the way they did, at face value.

3 The various examples detailed in this chapter make clear that relatively subtle conditioning can be powerful in eliciting behaviour change. On a cautionary

note, it can be difficult to enact broader and more sustained behavioural change with these types of interventions.

4 The idea that personality is learnt through experience does not sit well with the notion of personality as an internal construct. However, psychological behaviourism provides researchers with a theoretical framework in which to consider the interplay between environmental stimulus, biology and psychological factors.

3.4.6 References/further reading

Giné, X., Karlan, D., and Zinman, J. (2010). Put Your Money Where Your Butt Is: A Commitment Contract for Smoking Cessation. *American Economic Journal: Applied Economics*, 2 (4), pp. 213–235.

Pavlov, I. P. (1902; reprint, 2014). *The Work of the Digestive Glands*. Miami: Hard Press Publishing.

Skinner, B. F. (1938; reprint, 2006). *The Behavior of Organisms: An Experimental Analysis*. New York: Copley Publishing Group.

Staats, A. W. (1996). *Behavior and Personality: Psychological Behaviorism*. New York: Springer.

Watson, J. B., and Rayner, R. (1920). Conditioned Emotional Reactions. *Journal of Experimental Psychology*, 3(1), pp. 1–14.

More information about the Lowe's Pay & Save nudge experiments can be found in the following article:

Moss, M. (2013). Nudged to the Produce Aisle by a Look in the Mirror. *The New York Times*, 27th August. https://www.nytimes.com/2013/08/28/dining/wooing-us-down-the-produce-aisle.html [accessed 05/03/2021].

Below are links to the Müller Light and Virgin Media adverts:

Müller Light (2020). *Müllerlight Greek Style Advert Featuring Katarina Johnson-Thompson*. https://www.youtube.com/watch?v=MZzToh_ypVA [accessed 25/04/2021].

Virgin Media (2019). *Switch to Super*. https://www.youtube.com/watch?v=3t2eERXcJUw [accessed 25/04/2021].

3.4.6.1 Want to know more?

If you wish to delve into more detail about classical and operant conditioning, the following book provides a detailed overview of theory and more recent application in an easily digestible format:

Domjan, M. (2004). *The Essentials of Conditioning and Learning*. American Psychological Association.

Chapter 4

How motivational forces drive behaviour

CHAPTER OVERVIEW

Key theories: hierarchy of needs, two-factor model, self-efficacy, expectancy theory, theory of planned behaviour, collective efficacy and cognitive dissonance.

4.1 We begin by looking at hierarchy of needs, which is generally considered to be one of the first structured models of motivation.

4.2 Next, a distinction is drawn between motivator and hygiene factors, where certain factors drive satisfaction and others result in dissatisfaction.

4.3 Following this, self-efficacy, that is, our belief in our ability to conduct a specific task, is discussed, along with considering the role of self-efficacy in expectancy theory and the theory of planned behaviour.

4.4 Next, we consider collective efficacy, that is our belief in the collective to conduct a specific task.

4.5 Finally, we look at the phenomenon of cognitive dissonance as a motivational force.

Introduction

The previous chapters state clearly that understanding human behaviour is a complex and challenging endeavour, with both social influence and personality playing a part in driving behavioural tendencies. If we are to consider why

DOI: 10.4324/9781003169932-4

people behave the way they do, we must also look at theories that model motivational forces. We are motivated by fundamental goals of survival and more abstract ones, about creative development and fulfilment. It follows that if we can understand what motivates people, then we can go some way to understanding behaviour.

There are many theories of motivation, and this field of human observation has remained a key area of interest to psychologists. Theories of motivation vary significantly in focus, method and, consequently, conclusions. As such, there is little consensus amongst academics; nonetheless, all theories have one thing in common, that is, the notion that human behaviour is in some sense organised and goal-directed.

Why are motivational forces important in behavioural research?

Motivational theory provides researchers with frameworks in which to explore motivations in different settings. It follows that if we can understand the factors that sit behind motivation, we can affect behavioural change. In this chapter, we will look at theories that detail the processes of motivation and those that seek to explain the emotions and cognitions that sit behind motivation.

In the beginning

Early explanations of motivation centred on instincts; for example, the American philosopher and psychologist William James was influenced by Charles Darwin's theory of natural selection and suggested a series of instincts, namely, fear, anger, love, shame and cleanliness. Perhaps unsurprisingly, motivation as an instinct is no longer considered valid. In the 1960s, Maslow's hugely influential hierarchy of needs curried favour.

4.1 Hierarchy of needs: determining physiological and higher-order needs

4.1.1 Defining hierarchy of needs

In the mid-20th century, psychologists were exploring the idea that we are motivated by a hierarchy of needs, starting with basic physiological needs extending to higher, more emotional needs. This approach was informed by the humanistic movement, in California, in the 1960s. Humanistic theory contends that both physiological and emotional needs are key motivational drivers. The emergence of the humanistic approach is an example of a paradigm shift, where unease about the emphasis on stimulus reinforcement in behaviourism and irritational thoughts in psychoanalysis, resulted in the advent of a new school of thought. A humanistic approach sits within the subjectivism research philosophy and makes three core existential assumptions:

1   We operate, to a greater or lesser extent, based on free will, which enables us to reach our potential.
2   We are innately good and seek to improve the world we live in. Whilst this does seem to be an overly optimistic view of humanity, it is about overcoming hardship, pain and despair.
3   We are motivated to be the best we can be, regarding psychological growth and fulfilment.

4.1.2 Reviewing hierarchy of needs theory

4.1.2.1 Abraham Maslow's hierarchy of needs

From studies of monkeys, Maslow observed that there is an order of needs, where the most basic physiological needs (e.g. breathing, water and warmth) must be met before higher needs can be addressed (Maslow, 1943, 1954). Needs are thought to be the motivators to behaviour, beyond basic physiological needs, Maslow suggested four further levels, starting with, safety, then love/well-being, esteem and finally self-actualisation or what Maslow later called transcendence.

Maslow argued that we operate between levels by a process of homeostasis. Whereby, if physiological needs are not met, then the needs of the above levels will be 'switched off'. Maslow referred to the needs at each level below self-actualisation as deficit-needs, whereby, if these needs are not met then there is a deficit. When the needs have been met then the motivational force is no longer in existence. As we develop, it is thought we progress up the levels, in theory, all the way to self-actualisation, although Maslow stated that not everyone would get to self-actualise. Maslow used different terms to explain this level, for instance, growth motivation which contrasts with the deficit motivation of the previous four levels. Additionally, Maslow referred to the needs at the uppermost level as being-needs, that is, needs that are necessary to ensure happiness, they include, morality, creativity, perfection and effortlessness. Should one be placed under extreme stress, it is possible to drop down to more basic survival-based levels. Interestingly, Maslow suggested that this could happen at not only an individual but a societal level. For instance, in times of war, a society might function at a basic safety or physiological level and only move up a level when the environmental conditions are much improved.

Typically, Maslow's hierarchy of needs is represented by a triangle (or pyramid) that is aesthetically pleasing and seemingly intuitive. However, the triangle might not be the best representation of Maslow's model. Intriguingly, at no point did Maslow frame his ideas with a triangle. It is not clear exactly when the triangle came into being, probably from the business/management community in the 1960s. Whilst this does not invalidate the triangle as such, it might help to explain some of the criticisms that have been levelled against Maslow's theory. The triangle, with clear horizontal demarcation for different need levels, suggests that one must meet all the needs of each level below before progressing to the next level. It also suggests that we focus on one need at a time and that these needs follow the same order for all of us. Another problem with the triangle is that it suggests that there is an end point to growth. Interestingly, Maslow himself argued that we can have needs partially met at different levels of the hierarchy.

4.1.2.1.1 WHAT ABOUT A LADDER?

It has been suggested that a ladder might serve as a better representation of Maslow's theory rather than a triangle, as illustrated in Figure 4.1.

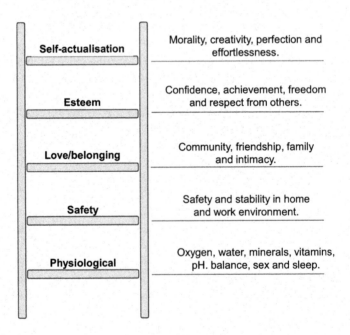

Figure 4.1 Maslow's hierarchy of needs 'ladder'

The ladder confers a number of advantages over the triangle. Notwithstanding a few representations of the triangle as a mountain, it is difficult to imagine someone climbing a triangle. It is not so difficult to imagine someone climbing a ladder. Whilst climbing the ladder, it is possible to occupy different parts with our hands and feet, thus addressing needs at different levels simultaneously. Further, we can climb not only up, but down the ladder, should the need arise. It will be interesting to see if over time the academic community and those in wider management circles adopt the ladder or stick steadfastly to the triangle.

4.1.2.2 Clayton Alderfer's ERG theory

Alderfer's theory of motivation (1969) builds on the work of Maslow and proposes three rather than five hierarchical levels, namely, existence, relatedness and growth (ERG). As in the case of Maslow's model, the ERG model is often depicted as a triangle. This brings into play the same issues seen with using a triangle to illustrate Maslow's model. Alderfer's model assumes that the order of needs will be different for different people. In addition to this key distinction, the assumption is that needs are not always progressive. Alderfer's theory is also a little more rational than Maslow's model; for instance, sex is no longer in the basic need level, as it is not seen as crucial to an individual's existence. In Table 4.1, the key elements of Alderfer's model are presented.

4.1.2.2.1 FRUSTRATION-REGRESSION PRINCIPLE

Alderfer argued that in satisfying higher needs, the reward becomes more intense, akin to a form of addiction. Alderfer suggested that if we are unable to fulfil a need, we become frustrated and regress to a lower level to remove that frustration. In other words, in Alderfer's model, people can move up and down levels.

Table 4.1 Alderfer's ERG model

Level	Definition
Growth needs	• Realising our potential including intellectual and creative growth.
Relatedness	• Relationships including family, friends and work colleagues.
Existence needs	• Physical well-being including food, warmth, the air that we breathe and so on.

Hierarchy of needs theory is used extensively in marketing and management circles for the following reasons:

■ The theory is undeniably simple, it is easy to understand and, consequently, straightforward to apply to different settings.
■ The theory presents the drivers of behaviour as dynamic and changing.
■ The theory considers physical, emotional, social and intellectual factors and how they impact on behaviour.
■ Whilst self-actualisation is not a desired goal for many, belonging and self-esteem are key components of our sense of self and identity.
■ The theory can be applied at an individual or group level.

4.1.3 Measuring hierarchy of needs in behavioural research

4.1.3.1 Pyramid-building

For some participants, the notion of a hierarchy of needs can seem a little abstract. In a qualitative setting, asking participants to build a pyramid can help to make the task more relatable. This technique works well when discussing different purchase drivers. For example, participants are given paper cups and asked to write on the cups different needs that come to mind when thinking about a particular product. Next, participants must build the pyramid. The value in this task is not simply the pyramid but unpacking the rationale for the building process.

4.1.3.2 Sorting task

The three levels of the ERG model can be operationalised in research using a structured sorting task. Participants are asked to write down needs when thinking about a particular product or service. Next, participants are asked to sort the needs into growth, relatedness and existence needs. Participants are then asked to explain the outcomes of the sorting task. This can be conducted as a group exercise or at an individual level. Changing the names of each level so they are more relatable will help participants better comprehend the task; for example, identification (growth), emotional value (relatedness) and functional value (existence).

4.1.3.3 Quantitative measurement

Hierarchy of needs can be measured using a set of behavioural or attitudinal scales. The exact question set will depend on the research setting. For example, in Table 4.2, key question areas in an occupational setting are presented.

As noted earlier, hierarchy of needs theory can be applied at both an individual and societal level. In Table 4.3, question areas for societal needs are detailed.

Table 4.2 Occupational hierarchy of needs question areas

Level	Question area
Self-actualisation	• Growth, individual development and empowerment.
Esteem	• Self-image and recognition from team members.
Belonging / love	• Social acceptance from peer group and cooperation on the job.
Safety	• Supportive work practices.
Physiological	• Salary and stable employment.

Table 4.3 Society hierarchy of needs question areas

Level	Question area
Self-actualisation	• Educational obtainment.
Esteem	• Human rights, democracy, free will and employment.
Belonging/love	• Divorce, infant mortality rate and community cohesion.
Safety	• Safety from war/conflict, safety from crime and life expectancy.
Physiological	• Diet and GDP per person.

4.1.4 Hierarchy of needs theory in action

4.1.4.1 British Airways brand review

From a market research perspective, Maslow's hierarchy of needs is a useful tool in which to explore the needs of consumers from basic physiological needs to more complex emotional needs. Let us look now at the application of hierarchy of needs to brand loyalty. Although Maslow never envisaged his model being used to explore brand, the concepts of physiology, safety, belonging, self-esteem and self-actualisation can be used to identify why people demonstrate commitment to different brands, as illustrated in Figure 4.2.

In this study, hierarchy of needs theory was used to explore different carriers, including British Airways, EasyJet and Virgin Atlantic. Focus groups were conducted with short- and long-haul travellers. In Figure 4.3, the brand loyalty drivers for British Airways are presented, where the attributes of the brand are detailed from the physical aspects of the proposition extending to cognitive and affective attributes.

As can be seen, the British Airways brand is interwoven with perceived values of what it is to be 'British'. Interestingly, in 1997 British Airways launched a new brand image, that was intended to turn the perception of the brand from a British airline to a global airline that just happens to have its headquarters in Britain. To

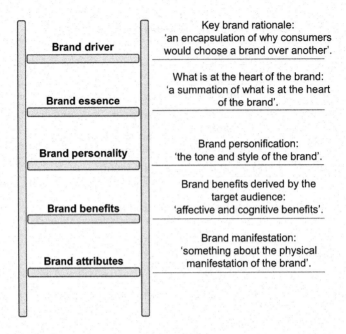

Figure 4.2 Brand loyalty drivers

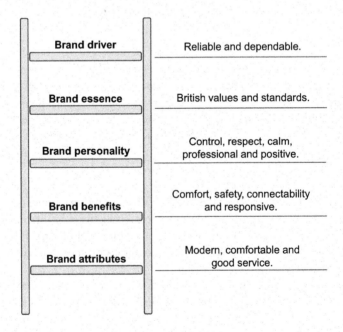

Figure 4.3 Brand engineering model example

communicate this vision, the tail fins of the aeroplanes were painted with different world images. The media and public's responses were mixed; whilst it was liked by some, others were perplexed and many actively disliked the rebranding. The problem was, whilst it was acknowledged that the airline was genuinely an international company, it was seen by the British public as quintessentially British. Reflecting its British roots, two years later the world images gave way to a design of the union flag.

4.1.4.2 Social media engagement

Hierarchy of needs can be used to understand basic lower-order needs to cognitive and affective needs when considering social media engagement. In the study below, one-to-one interviews were conducted amongst active social media users. The results are presented in Figure 4.4.

The start point is ensuring that there is a reliable connection to social media apps. Today, we take it for granted that at any time, day or night, we can check our social media feeds, post a message, or upload a video. Assuming our most basic needs are met, we then turn to safety. On social media, this is about protecting our privacy; we set up profiles and load personal information and trust social media companies to securely store our data. Next, our ability to connect with others, such as joining groups and private connections, is important. How we feel about what we do in these apps is important in developing and maintaining a positive

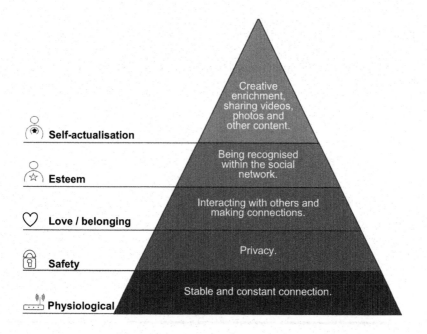

Figure 4.4 Social media engagement

self-image. Self-actualisation is about creative fulfilment; for instance, we might make connections with similar-minded people that help create and share new ideas and knowledge. The results from this study suggest that to meet higher-order needs, social media users must be free to express themselves creatively.

4.1.4.3 Electric car manufacturer brand analysis

In this study, the ERG model is used to unpack product/brand value drivers for different car manufacturers. Before engaging in primary research, the three levels of the model were translated into question areas, as detailed in Table 4.4.

Focus groups were conducted amongst car owners in Great Britain, France and Germany. Using the above question areas, participants were asked to identify key characteristics that were important to them when considering different car brands. Next, participants were asked to sort the key characteristics into the three value levels. The task was repeated for different car brands. The results for Tesla, the American electric car manufacturer, are presented in Figure 4.5.

Table 4.4 Aligning ERG to brand values

Level	Question area
Identification value (Growth)	• What are the intrinsic values? (e.g. kind, warm, responsible, modern, egalitarian and individual).
Emotional value (Relatedness)	• How does it make you feel? (e.g. reduces anxiety, makes me happy, empowers, is fun, is attractive, inspires and is rewarding).
Functional value (Existence)	• Does it meet a fundamental purpose or goal? (e.g. enables, simplifies, saves time and reduces effort).

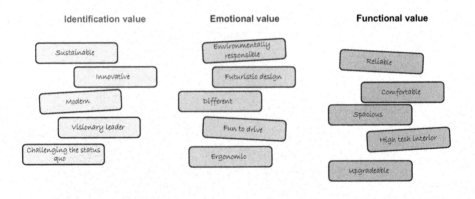

Figure 4.5 Tesla ERG model

On completion of the sorting task, respondents were asked to talk through the outcomes of that task:

■ Functional value: at the functional level, the physical attributes of the car are important, both in terms of key features of the car and assumed reliability and safety.
■ Emotional value: often more ethereal qualities of the car create emotional value, such as how the car feels to drive or whether it was aesthetically designed.
■ Identification value: a strong position as innovative, coupled with links to SpaceX and The Boring Company, headed up by the entrepreneur, Elon Musk, helps create a strong brand identity.

As can be seen, the Tesla brand is in the enviable position of having a very strong value proposition from the functional aspects of the cars right through to the identification value level of the brand. It must be acknowledged that not all brands will get beyond the functional and emotional levels.

4.1.5 Implications for behavioural research

1   Hierarchy of needs models look at physical, emotional, social and intellectual factors and present these as dynamic and changing motivational forces.
2   Distinguishing between physiological and more abstract emotional needs can provide powerful insights into how best to position a brand along with informing the development of compelling and relevant marketing messages.
3   Hierarchy models of motivation are relatively simple and easy to use, and they can be applied to different settings, as illustrated by the various examples detailed in this chapter. Further, the theory can be applied at an individual and societal level.
4   A hierarchy of needs can seem a little abstract; both pyramid-building and sorting tasks help to make the task of constructing a hierarchy of needs more relatable for participants.

4.1.6 References/further reading

Alderfer, C. P. (1969). An Empirical Test of a New Theory of Human Needs. *Organizational Behavior and Human Performance*, 4 (2), pp. 142–175.
Maslow, A. H. (1954; reprint, 1987). *Motivation and Personality*. TBS.
Maslow, A. H. (1943). A Theory of Human Motivation. *Psychological Review*, 50 (4), pp. 370–396.

The text below provides more detail on Maslow's work.
Maslow, A. H. (1962; reprint, 2011). *Towards the Psychology of Being*. Radford: Wilder
    Publications.

4.2 Two-factor theory: addressing motivational and hygiene factors

4.2.1 Defining motivator and hygiene factors

In the occupational environment, there are factors that motivate and those that demotivate, which have come to be known as motivator and hygiene factors, respectively. As a rule of thumb, motivators lead to satisfaction and hygiene factors lead to dissatisfaction (as illustrated in Figure 4.6), whereby:

■ The opposite of job satisfaction is not dissatisfaction, but the absence of job satisfaction
■ The opposite of job dissatisfaction is not satisfaction, but the absence of job dissatisfaction

The notion of motivating and hygiene factors would suggest improving job satisfaction will not reduce dissatisfaction, and addressing job dissatisfaction will not result in satisfaction. As such, the key to a harmonious workplace is to address motivators and hygiene factors in unison. Let us look now at the theory in this area of motivational research.

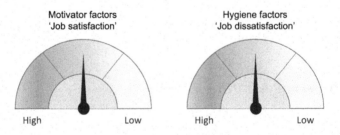

Figure 4.6 Job satisfaction and dissatisfaction

4.2.2 Reviewing motivator and hygiene theory

4.2.2.1 Frederick Herzberg's two-factor theory

In a similar vein to Maslow and Alderfer, the psychologist Herzberg (1959) believed that we are not content with meeting our basic physiological needs but strive for fulfilment of higher-order needs. Herzberg interviewed 200 engineers and accountants from 11 different companies in Pittsburgh, America. Herzberg and his colleagues observed that certain work attributes were motivational and resulted in satisfaction. Also, there was a separate group of work attributes that potentially demotivated and resulted in dissatisfaction. This led Herzberg to suggest a distinction between motivators and hygiene factors, as illustrated in Figure 4.7.

According to Herzberg, motivator and hygiene factors address two distinct needs. Hygiene factors relate to physiological needs about pay and conditions and motivator factors relate to psychological needs about growth and fulfilment. As such, motivator and hygiene factors can be aligned to Maslow's hierarchy of needs, as illustrated in Figure 4.8.

Herzberg's model suggests that to motivate employees, employers must recognise that both motivator and hygiene factors are at play. As illustrated in Figure 4.9, there are four possible motivational states.

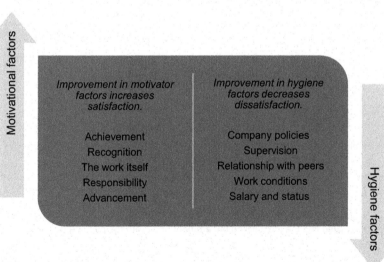

Figure 4.7 Motivator and hygiene factors

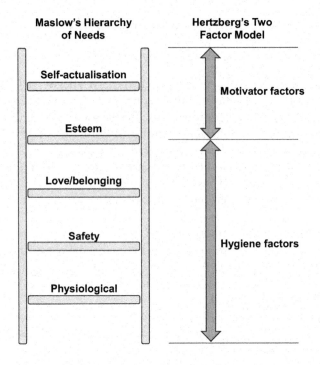

Figure 4.8 Motivator and hygiene factors aligned to Maslow's hierarchy of needs

High hygiene and
high motivation

• Employees have few, if any grievances and are highly motivated.
• This is the best-case scenario.

High hygiene and
low motivation

• Employees have few, if any grievances, although they are not highly motivated.
• Employees are simply turning up for the pay.

Low hygiene and
high motivation

• Employees have many grievances but are highly motivated.
• Employees find the job fulfilling but are not happy with the pay and conditions.

Low hygiene and
low motivation

• Employees have many grievances and are not motivated.
• This is the worst-case scenario.

Figure 4.9 Motivator and hygiene factors scenarios

There are a few criticisms of Hertzberg's two-factor theory that we need to be mindful of:

■ The theory ignores the situational context in which motivational forces operate.
■ The theory is based on engineers and accountants and thus lacks ecological validity (the extent to which the findings can be generalised to real-world settings).
■ What might be one person's motivator might be another's hygiene factor. For example, pay and conditions demotivate some employees but motivate others.
■ There is no overall objective measure of satisfaction.

Notwithstanding the above criticisms, Herzberg's two-factor theory is widely used in management circles and provides a practical framework in which to design working practices that engender satisfaction and abate dissatisfaction.

4.2.3 Measuring motivator and hygiene factors in behavioural research

Many different scales have been developed over time. However, in order that the measure be effective, it will need to be configured to the specific workplace setting under inspection.

Question areas that address motivator factors should include:

■ Achievement recognition.
■ Ability to learn.
■ Feeling appreciated.
■ Being given challenges.
■ Being able to grow and develop.
■ Having a sense of accomplishment.

Question areas that address hygiene factors should include:

■ Job security.
■ Support and relationship with supervisors.
■ Salary and package.
■ Working conditions.
■ Views of fellow colleagues.

4.2.4 Motivator and hygiene theory in action

4.2.4.1 Measuring retail staff commitment

The application of Herzberg's two-factor model is largely within the field of employee management. In the example detailed below, research was conducted to identify key motivator and demotivator factors of employees for a major European retail brand. The company was cognisant of the importance of addressing factors that not only drove satisfaction but those that result in dissatisfaction. It was observed that unhappy staff do not perform well, are often absent and tend not stay with the company very long. An employee survey was administered to staff at all levels. Motivator and hygiene factors were identified. The importance of each factor in driving commitment (measured as a correlation) was plotted against stated commitment. As can be seen in Figure 4.10, hygiene factors are important to some extent in driving commitment, but the contribution levels off; in contrast, motivator factors are key to driving commitment to the organisation.

In response to the research findings, the retailer sought to address both motivational and hygiene factors, as detailed overleaf.

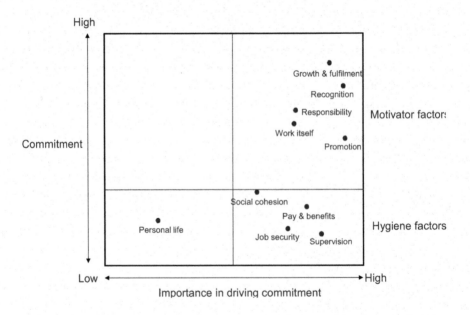

Figure 4.10 Commitment and hygiene and motivator factors

To encourage job satisfaction:

■ Training was reviewed to help support personal development.
■ A greater emphasis was placed on recognising individual and team achievements throughout the organisation.

To address possible job dissatisfaction:

■ Staff were encouraged to delegate decision-making authority to empower staff working below them.
■ A more supportive and collegiate working culture was encouraged.
■ Pay and conditions were benchmarked against other retail companies.
■ Company rules that were considered petty and bureaucratic were updated.

The employment survey was repeated a year later, levels of satisfaction had improved and dissatisfaction was lower. Further, absenteeism and staff turnover were markedly down from that observed in the previous year.

4.2.5 Implications for behavioural research

1   Herzberg's theory makes clear that in the workplace there are two distinct human needs. Hygiene factors relate to physiological needs about pay and conditions and motivator factors relate to psychological needs about growth and fulfilment.
2   The theory suggests that the opposite of satisfaction is not dissatisfaction and that employers need to consider how to best engender satisfaction whilst addressing possible dissatisfaction.
3   Although Herzberg came up with his theory in the 1960s, his theory remains important in the field of employee management to this day.

4.2.6 References/further reading

Herzberg, F., Mausner, B., and Snyderman, B. (1959). *The Motivation to Work* (2nd ed.). New York: John Wiley.

4.2.6.1 Want to know more?

A more detailed review of Herzberg's two-factor theory can be found in the following text:

Herzberg, F. (1968). One More Time: How Do You Motivate Employees? *Harvard Business Review*, 46 (1), pp. 53–62.

4.3 Self-efficacy: harnessing the power of self-belief

4.3.1 Defining self-efficacy

Self-efficacy refers to an individual's belief in their ability to organise and perform a task successfully. An individual's self-efficacy will influence how they cope with the challenges they face in everyday life. Given this, self-efficacy affects most forms of behaviour and as such, is a key motivational force.

4.3.2 Reviewing self-efficacy theory

4.3.2.1 Albert Bandura's self-efficacy

The term self-efficacy is credited to Bandura (1982) and is defined as an individual's judgement on how well they think they can execute a task. Like personality traits discussed earlier, self-efficacy can be considered as a dimension where participants load somewhere between strong and weak efficacy poles, as illustrated in Figure 4.11.

4.3.2.1.1 RECIPROCAL DETERMINISM

Self-efficacy is central to Bandura's social learning theory (1977) which deals with reciprocal determinism and how we learn through social experience. Bandura was concerned with explaining behaviour in different settings and argued that an individual's behaviour is influenced not only by the social environment but also by the individual who influences the social environment. This is referred to as reciprocal determinism, which is thought to be product of the interplay of behaviour, environment and personal factors as detailed below:

- Behaviour refers to anything we do in the pursuit of a goal; a positive outcome will make the behaviour more likely and a negative outcome, less likely.
- The environment refers to things external to us, the context in which behaviour is originated and sustained and includes not just our physical environment but also our social environment.

Strong self efficacy	Weak self efficacy
• Treat challenges as something to conquer.	• Go out of their way to avoid challenges.
• Believe they can achieve what they want.	• Tend not to believe they can achieve what they want.
• Deal with setbacks in their stride.	• Focus on personal failures.
• Exhibit a keen interest in the challenges they face.	• Exhibit little interest in the challenges they face.

Figure 4.11 Self-efficacy dimension

■ Personal factors refer to things about the person, for instance, emotions, beliefs and values.

As can be seen, Bandura acknowledges the importance of positive and negative conditioning but adds personal factors and the environment into the mix. These factors interact to create a reciprocal effect. For instance, a nervous flyer might act in an agitated and unpredictable way in a plane. Depending on personal factors, this will make other passengers on the plane feel ill at ease, and some might even become annoyed with the nervous flyer for making a fuss. In this instance, the behaviour of the nervous flyer has influenced the environment, and in turn, the behaviour of the fellow passengers will have an impact on the nervous flyer and so on.

4.3.2.1.2 FOUR WAYS TO INFLUENCE SELF-EFFICACY

The belief in our ability to achieve the desired outcome will naturally be impacted by reciprocal determinism. That is, behaviour, the social environment and personal factors will be key in shaping self-efficacy. Let us look at this in more detail; according to Bandura, through experience we learn, based on mastery, observation, physiology and verbal persuasion, as illustrated in Table 4.5.

Table 4.5 Influencers on self-efficacy

Influencers	Definition
1 Mastery	• The response as a product of conducting a specific task. • If we repeatedly carry out a task successfully then we will develop a strong self-efficacy, based on the expectation of success. • Conversely, continued failure at a task will likely result in a low self-efficacy, based on expectations of failure.
2 Observation	• Observational learning does not require behaviour on the observer's part, only the observations of others, but nonetheless can be equally effective in driving motives. • If we observe someone completing a task successfully it will improve our self-efficacy. • Conversely, observing others failing will have the opposite effect, lowering our self-efficacy.
3 Physiology	• Physiology refers to our emotional state at the time. • We experience different states of emotional arousal, how we interpret this influences the extent to which we have a strong self-efficacy, or not. For instance, removing stress will help improve self-efficacy.
4 Verbal persuasion	• Encouraging or discouraging verbal messages from those around us. • Verbal persuasion is generally thought to be the weakest influence on self-efficacy, although, the more credible the source, the greater the influence.

4.3.2.1.3 AN ADDITIONAL FIFTH WAY TO INFLUENCE TO SELF-EFFICACY

The psychologist James Maddux dedicated his career to the study of self-efficacy and goal-setting and suggested a fifth influencer (Maddux, 1995), which he called imaginal experiences, as illustrated in Table 4.6.

In sum, Bandura and Maddux's influencers will, to a greater or lesser degree, impact on our sense of self-efficacy.

4.3.2.1.4 SELF-REGULATORY PROCESSES

According to Bandura, there are a number of self-regulatory processes at play, that is, processes that help to activate and sustain behaviour and, therefore, impact on self-efficacy. As illustrated in Table 4.7, Bandura suggested three steps.

As can be seen, we regulate behaviour in the pursuit of a goal. We ensure that behaviour aligns with our internally held benchmarks, and then we reflect upon the behaviour outcomes and consider possible next steps. As we reflect, the belief that we have learned and achieved a positive outcome will help to drive self-efficacy.

Table 4.6 Influencers on self-efficacy

Influencers	Definition
5 Imaginal experiences	• The art of visualising yourself behaving effectively or successfully in a given situation. • To enhance our self-efficacy, we need to paint a picture of ourselves in a favourable position.

Table 4.7 Bandura's self-regulatory steps

Interactions	Definition
Self-observation	• The process of observing our own behaviour.
Judgment	• The process of making judgements based on what we see. We compare and contrast against what we consider to be an acceptable outcome. • Prior to engaging in a task, we will have some sense of what we want to achieve, it is likely that this will constitute a benchmark.
Self-response	• In comparing outcomes with the assumed benchmark, we can infer how well we have done. • A successful outcome might result in a feeling of pride or self-worth.

4.3.2.2 Victor H. Vroom's expectancy theory

Self-efficacy is a key component of Vroom's expectancy theory. Vroom (1964) defines motivation as a process governing choice. Expectancy theory details the mental processes that allow us to make decisions/choices. Like Bandura, Vroom suggests that there is a relationship between behaviour and outcome, but additionally, brings into play the notion of effort as a core driver of motivation. Expectancy theory suggests that if we believe there is a positive association between effort and performance, then a favourable outcome will occur. Behaviour is thought to be a product of not only the perception of effort for a specific task, but the perception of effort in possible alternative actions. In other words, motivation is a product of comparing and contrasting the extent of effort that is required.

Against this backdrop, Vroom's model consists of three factors, which are a combination of attitudes and values, as illustrated in Table 4.8.

Expectancy theory suggests that when deciding one behaviour over another, we select a behaviour with the greatest motivational force, which is expressed as follows:

Motivational Force = (Effort X Performance X Utility)

In the above equation, the multiplier ensures that only when all three factors are high will the motivation force be high. Further, if any one factor is low or close to zero, irrespective of other scores, the motivational score will be low. For instance, if an employee believes that their effort will lead to performance, then motivational force will only be strong if the reward is sufficiently valued.

Table 4.8 Expectancy theory dimensions

Factors	Definition
Effort	• Self-efficacy: the belief that the desired outcome will happen. • Task difficulty: the perceived difficulty of a task, difficult tasks are likely to result in high perceived effort. • Perceived control: the extent to which one feels able to control the expected outcome, low perceived control will result in low expectancy.
Performance	• The belief that performance will result in the intended reward.
Utility	• The value ascribed to the outcome of behaviour, based on beliefs, values and emotions. • This is not satisfaction, but the expected satisfaction of a particular outcome.

4.3.2.3 Icek Ajzen's theory of planned behaviour

Self-efficacy is also a key component of the theory of planned behaviour (Ajzen 1985, 1991). The theory proposes that intentions are key to predicting behaviour. Intentions are seen as a product of attitudes towards a behaviour, subjective norms and perceived behavioural control, as detailed in Table 4.9. As can be seen, perceived behavioural control refers to the degree to which an individual believes they can perform a behaviour and is derived from Bandura's concept of self-efficacy.

The theory of planned behaviour is one of the most widely applied models of behaviour change and is used in healthcare, along with advertising and sports psychology.

4.3.3 Measuring self-efficacy in behavioural research

4.3.3.1 Qualitative immersion

As noted earlier, self-efficacy is about a belief in our ability to organise and perform a task successfully. In a qualitative setting, the following question areas should be explored:

■ Problem-solving.
■ Ability to deal with unexpected events/situations.
■ Calmness under stress.
■ Resourcefulness.
■ Perseverance.

Table 4.9 Intention factors

Factors	Definition
Attitudes towards a behaviour	• Attitudes towards a behaviour that are positive are much more likely to result in an 'intention' to act.
Subjective norms	• The normative expectations of others (in the social groups we occupy) to perform a specific act (refer to Section 1.1 for a more detailed review of normative influence). • Strong normative influence is much more likely to result in an intention to act.
Perceived behavioural control (~ self-efficacy)	• The degree to which an individual believes they can perform a behaviour. • A strong perceived behavioural control is more likely to result in an 'intention' to act.

Asking participants to give examples of situations where they have needed to solve a problem/complete a task, can help in understanding the nature of self-efficacy.

4.3.3.2 Quantitative measurement

There are many different measures of self-efficacy. Schwarzer and Jerusalem's general self-efficacy scale (1995) is one of the most cited. It is a self-reported questionnaire, consisting of ten questions using a four-point agreement scale. This is a general efficacy scale; for specific settings, questions will need to be tailored to the context of the research.

4.3.4 Self-efficacy theory in action

4.3.4.1 Enabling positive health outcomes

Self-efficacy has been a key tool in encouraging positive health outcomes. Below are examples where self-efficacy has been used to change behaviour:

- Condom use.
- Maintaining an exercise regime.
- Reducing alcohol consumption.
- Giving up smoking.
- Encouraging breastfeeding.
- Managing chronic pain.
- Following a healthy diet.

Below we look at an example of reciprocal determinism in the healthcare profession.

4.3.4.2 Understanding patient-doctor dependency

A pharmaceutical company wished to better understand the nature of the patient-doctor relationships and how best to develop effective treatment protocols for Type 2 diabetes. One-to-one interviews were conducted with doctors and adult patients in the United Kingdom, Spain, France and Germany. Some of the patients reported doctor dependency, and this typically resulted in the patient persistently consulting the doctor, refusing to see other doctors in the practice or specialists relative to the patient's condition. In Table 4.10, patient and doctor behaviours that contributed to a dependent relationship are presented.

Those that were less dependent, tended to demonstrate a stronger sense of self-efficacy and report more self-reliant behaviours in managing Type 2 diabetes.

Table 4.10 Factors impacting on doctor-dependency

Actor	Factors
Patient	• Reported complications from the disease. • Reported unexplained symptoms. • Had difficulty relating to people in social settings. • Were depressed and/or anxious and involved. • Demonstrated emotional attachment to the doctor. • Had limited faith in specialists.
Doctor	• Not setting clear planning goals • Not communicating the operating parameters of the relationship. • Not demonstrating what is achievable and what is not.

Intriguingly, whether dependent or not, doctors adjust their style of engagement to accommodate the patient's orientation, which in turn results in changes in patient behaviour, thus demonstrating reciprocal determinism. Dependency was reduced when doctors sought to empower patients through education about Type 2 diabetes, involved patients more in the treatment decisions and offered counselling and support when there were wider mental issues at play.

Below is an example of applying expectancy theory.

4.3.4.3 Encouraging retail loyalty scheme participation

In market research, we are often tasked with testing a new product or service and seek to ascertain the likely engagement drivers and possible uptake. To do this, we need to address effort, performance and utility. In this example, focus groups were conducted amongst consumers to identify motivational forces and likely participation in a new retail loyalty scheme. The perceived effort was instrumental in ensuring that not only do people sign up in the first place but that they continue to participate in the loyalty scheme over time. Additionally, how well the scheme performs will be of the utmost importance; a scheme that is overly complex is unlikely to engage. Finally, the value of the reward must be proportionate to the perceived effort required, as illustrated in Figure 4.12.

Below, is an example of applying the theory of planned behaviour.

4.3.4.4 Clothing retailer online launch

An established high street clothing retailer was looking at launching an online proposition. Focus groups were conducted amongst existing and prospective

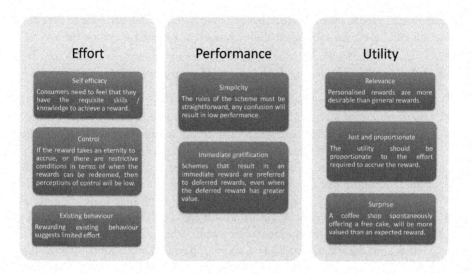

Figure 4.12 Loyalty scheme motivational forces

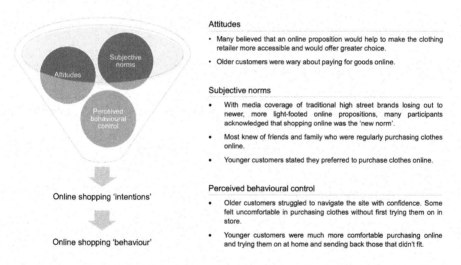

Figure 4.13 Intentions to shop online

customers to understand intentions and likely behaviour. In Figure 4.13, the results from the focus groups are presented.

The research makes clear that there are a number of barriers to converting older customers to online services. Possible solutions to these barriers include installing in-store tablets where staff can take customers through searching for products along with helping customers through an online purchase. Offering customers discounts and incentives to purchase online was also considered as a conversion tactic.

4.3.5 Implications for behavioural research

1 Self-efficacy refers to an individual's belief in their ability to organise and perform a task successfully. It follows that if we do not believe we will succeed at a specific task, the chances of us trying is greatly reduced. Given this, self-efficacy is an important motivational force in market research.

2 Mastery, observation, physiology, verbal persuasion and imaginal experiences are all important determinants of self-efficacy. By understanding the determinants of self-efficacy, researchers will have a more informed understanding of the nature and power of this motivational force.

3 Self-efficacy is a key component of expectancy theory. Expectancy theory provides a practical framework in which to understand motivational forces. The theory suggests that the interplay between performance, effort and utility is important to driving behaviour.

4 In the theory of planned behaviour, self-efficacy is represented as perceived behavioural control and coupled with attitudes and subjective norms provides researchers with a mechanism in which to understand intentions that sit behind behaviour in different settings.

4.3.6 References/further reading

Ajzen, I. (1985). *From Intentions to Actions: A Theory of Planned Behavior*. In J. Kuhl and J. Beckmann (Eds.), *Action Control: From Cognition to Behavior*, pp. 11–39. Berlin, Heidelber, New York: Springer-Verlag.

Ajzen, I. (1991). The Theory of Planned Behavior. *Organizational Behavior and Human Decision Processes*, 50 (2), pp. 179–211.

Bandura, A. (1977). *Social Learning Theory*. Englewood Cliffs, NJ: Prentice Hall.

Bandura, A. (1982). Self-Efficacy Mechanism in Human Agency. *American Psychologist*, 37 (2), pp. 122–147.

Maddux, J. E. (Ed.) (1995). Self-Efficacy, Adaptation, and Adjustment: Theory, Research, and Application. *Springer Science & Business Media*. Windsor.

Schwarzer, R., and Jerusalem, M. (1995). Generalized Self-Efficacy Scale. In J. Weinman, S. Wright, and M. Johnston (Eds.), *Measures in Health Psychology: A user's portfolio. Causal and Control Beliefs*, pp. 35–37. Windsor: NFER-NELSON.

Vroom, V. H. (1964). *Work and Motivation*. Oxford, England: Wiley.

4.3.6.1 Want to know more?

Most introductory to psychology textbooks will discuss self-efficacy. For a more detailed review see below:
Bandura, A. (1997). *Self-Efficacy: The Exercise of Control*. New York: W.H.Freeman and Company.

4.4 Collective efficacy: achieving shared goals

4.4.1 Defining collective efficacy

In the previous chapter, we looked at self-efficacy as a motivational force. In considering the power of efficacy, we must consider efficacy at a group or society level. This is known as collective efficacy and is a phenomenon of interest to psychologists and sociologists alike. Psychologists look at the process of collective efficacy, whilst sociologist look at the importance of collective efficacy in different social settings.

4.4.2 Reviewing collective efficacy theory

Collective efficacy was first coined by Bandura (1997), where efficacy is in relation to a group's belief in their ability to achieve a shared goal or task. Although many tasks that we carry out are as an individual, there are many that we do as a shared experience, where we work together to achieve a shared goal. For instance, we might play in a Saturday football team, be part of a neighbourhood watch scheme, work with colleagues to deliver an important project, these are all examples of working in groups where there will be, to a greater or lesser extent, a sense of collective efficacy.

4.4.2.1 Collective and self-efficacy reciprocity

Collective efficacy is inextricably linked to self-efficacy. If there are many self-doubters in a group, collective efficacy is likely to be weak. Further, a strong performance by the group will inevitably result in strong self-efficacy.

4.4.2.2 The rise (and rise) of collective efficacy in western societies

Collective efficacy has become more important over time. Reasons for this include:

1 The decline in political and institutional trust: much has been written about this in recent years, where we have witnessed a move away from political and institutional trust, to a more community-based level of trust, this includes friends, family and work colleagues.
2 The demise of the expert: experts are no longer seen exclusively as the purveyors of knowledge; we now defer to non-experts within our immediate social sphere.
3 The role of technology as an enabler: technology has put the consumer at the centre stage for decision-making. For instance, it was not so long ago that an

editor of a newspaper would decide what the readership saw. Today, social networks enable the consumer to decide on content and argument.

4 The move away from corporate top-down management styles: management styles have progressively moved towards more heterarchical structures with an emphasis on the shared value of the employees.

5 An emphasis on human rights: movements such as LBGT+ have helped to foster more collective engagement.

4.4.2.3 *Influencers of collective efficacy*

All the above factors lead us towards ever greater collective decision-making. It follows that the same influencers that help inform self-efficacy are at play when considering collective efficacy. Mastery, observation, physiology, verbal persuasion and imaginal experiences, all operate at a group level. However, collective efficacy is thought only to occur when there is mutual trust and solidarity in a group.

4.4.3 Measuring collective efficacy in behavioural research

4.4.3.1 Quantitative measurement

Collective efficacy is typically discussed in terms of willingness of community members to intervene to help others. Within this definition, there has been much research amongst sociologists into the impact of collective efficacy and incidents of crime in neighbourhoods. This has resulted in the development of neighbourhood collective efficacy scales. For example, Sampson et al. (1997) developed a ten-item collective efficacy questionnaire. The questionnaire is designed to measure social cohesion and trust in neighbourhoods.

4.4.3.2 *Qualitative immersion*

Qualitatively, the following areas should be explored:

■ Extent of trust in the community.
■ The extent to which the community is seen to be close-knit.
■ The extent to which the community have shared values and beliefs.
■ Willingness to help fellow residents.
■ Willingness to intervene when there is unsocial or criminal behaviour.
■ Willingness to campaign on social issues affecting the community.
■ Evidence of role models for others to look up to.

For most other social settings, an effective question battery will need to address not only the aggregated belief in the group but also the perceived abilities of individuals within that group. A combination of these two measures will provide a reliable measure of collective efficacy.

4.4.4 Collective efficacy theory in action

4.4.4.1 Community spirit and adolescent obesity

Cohen et al. (2006) were concerned with whether there was a relationship between neighbourhood collective efficacy and levels of obesity in adolescents. Neighbourhood collective efficacy was a measure of willingness of community members to look out for each other and intervene if there was trouble in the community. Additionally, the study looked at the presence of adult role models and the extent to which there were shared community values and beliefs. The sample was drawn from 65 neighbourhoods in Los Angeles, America, with 807 adolescents and a further 3,000 adults. Adolescent obesity was obtained as a measure of BMI. It was found that there was a correlation between collective efficacy and BMI scores, where low community efficacy was associated with higher BMI scores. This study highlights the importance of directing healthcare interventions at a community level. For instance, intervention strategies should include group activities that help to develop and sustain collective efficacy.

4.4.4.2 Social and environmental influences on crime

In another study, Cohen et al. (2008) looked at the impact of social and environmental influences of collective efficacy. Data from the Los Angeles family and neighbourhood study and data about the environment, such as presence of parks, schools, bars and fast-food outlets, was analysed. It was found that the presence of parks within half a mile of the neighbourhood increased collective efficacy. Conversely, the prevalence of bars selling alcohol reduced collective efficacy. Areas with strong collective efficacy experienced lower levels of crime and individuals within those communities reported better health. The results of this study underline the importance of designing built social environments that help to foster collective efficacy.

4.4.4.3 Collective efficacy and educational attainment

Collective efficacy has also been considered regarding educational attainment in schools. It has been observed that the teacher's belief about the faculty's ability to organise and deliver the curriculum has a positive impact on students. That is, a strong sense of faculty efficacy is causally linked to education attainment. It has been suggested that collective teacher efficacy is a more powerful predictor of student achievement than student motivation, concentration, persistence and engagement (Hattie, 2016). Interestingly, where there is a strong collective efficacy amongst teachers, the school culture is characterised by high expectations of student attainment that, in turn, helps perpetuate success. This is likely to be a product of a self-fulfilling prophecy (as discussed in Section 2.5), where the teacher's expectations of their pupils help secure good grades.

4.4.5 Implications for behavioural research

1   Many of the decisions we make are not in isolation but are influenced by the wider groups we belong too. As such, collective efficacy is an important motivational force.
2   Collective efficacy is an area of research that has been neglected by the academic community. That said, it seems that in recent times collective efficacy has become ever more important.
3   Collective efficacy will inevitably impact on self-efficacy and vice versa. Given this, researchers should be cognisant of both forms of efficacy in seeking to explain behaviour.

4.4.6 References/further reading

Bandura, A. (1997). *Self-efficacy: The Exercise of Control.* New York: W.H. Freeman and Company.
Cohen, D. A., Finch, B. K., Bower, A., and Sastry, N. (2006). Collective Efficacy and Obesity: The Potential Influence of Social Factors on Health. *Social Science & Medicine,* 62, pp. 769–778.
Cohen, D. A., Finch, B. K., and Inagami, S. (2008). The Built Environment and Collective Efficacy. *Health & Place,* 14 (2), pp. 198–208.
Hattie, J. (2016). *Mindframes and Maximizers.* 3rd Annual Visible Learning Conference held in Washington, DC.
Sampson, R. J., Raudenbush, S. W., and Earls, F. (1997). Neighborhoods and Violent Crime: A Multilevel Study of Collective Efficacy. *Science,* 277 (5328), pp. 918–924.

4.5 Cognitive dissonance: addressing attitude and behaviour disharmony

4.5.1 Defining cognitive dissonance

Cognitive dissonance occurs when our attitudes and beliefs are not in harmony with our behaviour. This dissonance is thought to be discomforting, it can lead to anxiety, stress, regret or embarrassment, and consequently, we seek to reduce this apparent disharmony. For instance, we might feel bad about using plastic bags when shopping, having learnt that around eight million tonnes of plastic reach our oceans every year; to address this discomfort, we change our behaviour and start using reusable bags. In Aesop's fable *The Fox and the Grapes*, a fox spots a bunch of ripe grapes hanging from a vine and longs for them. The grapes are high up and the fox must jump up to the reach them, however, after many attempts it becomes clear they are simply out of reach. Rather than admit defeat, the fox post-rationalises that he did not want the grapes in the first place, thus reducing dissonance and resulting in the now-familiar idiom 'sour grapes.'

Clearly, the above is only a fable; that said, cognitive dissonance is an important phenomenon in market research. It is not uncommon for participants to post-rationalise behaviour where dissonance is in evidence. In this chapter, we discuss the theory of cognitive dissonance, look at strategies to reduce dissonance and examples of cognitive dissonance in action.

4.5.2 Reviewing cognitive dissonance theory

4.5.2.1 Leon Festinger's cognitive dissonance

The psychologist, Festinger argued that we seek harmony in attitudes, beliefs and behaviours. In *A Theory of Cognitive Dissonance* (1957), Festinger first coined the phrase cognitive dissonance, where it is suggested that when there is a contradiction between thoughts or beliefs and an individual's actions, there is dissonance.

4.5.2.1.1 CAUSES OF DISSONANCE

There are thought to be three causes of dissonance:

- Forced compliance: as we saw in Section 2.3, compliance is a form of conformity where we adhere to peer pressure to avoid conflict or censure. Although we might publicly change our behaviour, privately, we hold conflicting views.
- Marginal decision-making: when faced with a difficult decision where, say choosing A over B is at the margins, we might choose A but still hanker for B.
- Effort: if we expend a great deal of time and effort to achieve something without a positive outcome, then dissonance is likely.

The greater the discord between the belief and behaviour, the greater the dissonance. Beliefs that are personal and/or strongly held beliefs, tend to generate greater dissonance.

4.5.2.1.2 HOW TO REDUCE DISSONANCE

There are broadly three ways in which to reduce dissonance, as illustrated in Figure 4.14.

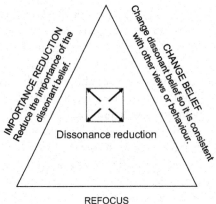

REFOCUS
Focus on supporting beliefs that outweigh the
dissonant belief.

Figure 4.14 Strategies to reduce dissonance

Take the example of smoking, we are all aware of the health implications of smoking. A smoker might argue that smoking helps them concentrate, gives them confidence when socialising and helps to calm them down when anxious or stressed. These are examples of refocusing on supporting beliefs that outweigh the dissonant belief. One might argue that the evidence that smoking is bad for you is greatly exaggerated; this is an example of reducing the importance of the dissonant belief. Changing the dissonant belief so that it is consistent with our views or behaviour is more challenging, it would require the smoker to give up smoking.

4.5.2.2 Buyer's Stockholm syndrome

Buyer's Stockholm syndrome is a form of cognitive dissonance, where buyers are held captive by their purchase decision. Unsurprisingly, post-purchase we are more likely to think positively about what we have purchased than negatively. It seems we make post-purchase rationalisations to justify the purchase and largely overlook the negatives. The causes of buyer's Stockholm syndrome are as follows:

■ We often make emotional decisions and rationalise them post hoc.
■ Misremembering is key, and typically we are unaware that we have made emotional decisions in the first place. We tend to remember the positives and downplay the negatives. The negative attributes of our choice can be ascribed to the product we did not choose.
■ Ownership matters: once we own something, we subscribe a higher value to it.

Imagine you were thinking about buying a new car, you know that the new model is due to come out soon, but you decide to seize the moment and buy the current model, even though you know the new car is better. In this instance, we will seek to rationalise the decision:

- Emotional investment: often, our decision to purchase a car is relatively emotional and instinctive in nature and we construct a 'rational' narrative to support that decision. Rationalised responses might include fuel economy, service costs, safety features and so on. However, the decision to buy the car might relate to more subjective and affective attributes, such as the aesthetic of the car or the manufacturer brand. Although probably not acknowledged, the influence of the salesperson would have also been key in the final decision.
- Ownership: owning the car and experiencing driving it helps reinforce our rationalised response to purchasing it in the first place.
- Misremembering: misremembering can take many forms; it can be as simple as forgetting key details or misattributing and suggesting that the old car is in some way better than the new one.

4.5.3 Measuring cognitive dissonance in behavioural research

It must be acknowledged that cognitive dissonance is a relatively subjective concept, and consequently, it can be difficult to objectively measure in market research. Measuring cognitive dissonance requires careful questioning regarding attitudes, beliefs and behaviour. For instance, if we were to address cognitive dissonance regarding product purchase, we might ask the following questions:

1   How happy are you with the decision you made?
2   Did you feel you purchased the right product?
3   Did you feel you got value for money?

For each of the above questions, it will be important to probe on the participant's answers to tease out the cognitive and affective components of their thinking. Here, the researcher should look for the tell-tale signs of dissonance-reduction techniques, including information reduction, changing belief and refocusing.

4.5.4 Cognitive dissonance theory in action

4.5.4.1 Cult behaviour and post rationalisations

The most famous example of cognitive dissonance can be found in Festinger's book *When Prophecy Fails* (1956). Festinger immersed himself in a UFO cult in Chicago, dubbed 'the seekers'. Festinger infiltrated the seekers with the goal of studying cognition and reactions when their beliefs failed to materialise. The cult leader prophesied the world would come to an end with a great flood on 21 December 1954. The cult leader claimed true believers would be rescued by a flying saucer from the planet Clarion. As a sign of their commitment, many from the cult had left their jobs, partners and given away any money they might have had. When the UFO did not materialise, many of the cult members convinced themselves that the UFO would come on Christmas eve, thus initially managing dissonance. However, dissonance was at its highest when the UFO did not materialise on Christmas eve. The cult members sat in stunned silence. Later, the cult leader stated that he had received a message that because of the good work of the cult members the God of earth had decided to spare the planet from destruction, providing the cult members with a way to reduce dissonance. Upon which, many packed up their things and headed home.

4.5.4.2 *Life insurance purchasing and post rationalisation*

Research suggests that whilst consumers attest to the importance of ensuring that there is financial provision for their family in the event of their death, many do not invest in life insurance. To deal with the obvious dissonance, consumers post-rationalise that the product is unaffordable and that it will not pay out should the worst happen, even though few have any facts or figures to support such notions. Often when presented with the monthly premium, consumers are pleasantly surprised at how low it is. Communicating the high level of payout across the industry also helps address commonly held beliefs that insurance companies do not pay out.

4.5.4.3 *Understanding bipartisan politics and climate change denialism*

Despite the scientific consensus on climate change, many remain unconvinced of the gravity of the situation. Moreover, some deny the very existence of climate change. Until recently, it was thought that this was a product of a lack of knowledge. However, studies have shown that knowledge is not causally related to beliefs about the environment. An alternative might be cognitive dissonance, where individuals seek to justify their beliefs about climate change based on several rationalisations:

■ The actions of one will not make a significant impact on climate change.
■ Climate change is a problem for third world countries rather than developed nations.
■ The impact of climate change has been exaggerated.
■ Climate change is not a product of human activity.

In America, climate change attitudes differ along partisan lines, where Democrats are more concerned about climate change than their Republican counterparts. A 2019 survey conducted by the Pew Research Group *US Public Views on Climate Change*, suggests that this disparity is growing ever greater. Also, there is disagreement about the causes of climate change, where Republicans are less convinced that climate change is a product of human activity. This might simply be a collective rationalisation by the Republicans to avoid possible dissonance. Intriguingly, trying to convince Republicans of the veracity of climate change is likely to lead to yet more dissonance (and result in further rationalisations), with the message being at odds with deeply held political and cultural beliefs. To put this in perspective, to accept climate change, the Republicans would have to abandon their staunch support of the power of the markets and economic growth, which based on the Pew Research findings, seems unlikely in the short term.

4.5.4.4 Individual differences

When considering cognitive dissonance, researchers should be mindful of confounding factors, such as age and personality disposition. As we get older, we are more likely to act on instinct, which increases the likelihood of dissonance (this may in part be a product of diminished memory). Some people are better able to cope with dissonance than others. Those that are anxious and involved tend to be more likely to suffer from dissonance. Those that demonstrate low levels of empathy tend to cope better with dissonance.

4.5.5 Implications for behavioural research

1 Cognitive dissonance is one of the more identifiable theories of psychology that can be applied to just about any attitude, belief and behaviour. Consequently, cognitive dissonance is a key motivational force.
2 Researchers should be mindful of the possibility that participants will employ strategies to reduce dissonance, including information reduction, changing belief and refocusing.
3 Cognitive dissonance is not always immediately observable and consequently, it can be difficult to objectively measure. However, with careful interviewing, it is possible to locate and understand dissonance.

4.5.6 References/further reading

Festinger, L (1957). *A Theory of Cognitive Dissonance*. Stanford, CA: Stanford University Press.
Festinger, L, Riecken, H. W., and Schachter. (1956; reprint, 2008). *When Prophecy Fails: A Social and Psychological Study of a Modern Group that Predicted the Destruction of the World*. London: Pinter & Martin.

Funk, C, and Hefferon, M. (2019). *US Public Views on Climate and Energy.* Pew Research Center, 25th November 2019. https://www.pewresearch.org/science/2019/11/25/u-s-public-views-on-climate-and-energy/ [accessed 21/12/2020].

4.5.6.1 Want to know more?

Cognitive dissonance is a theory that is discussed in depth by psychologists and non-academics alike. As such, there is much written about cognitive dissonance. For a critical review of the origins and more recent research, Joel Cooper's book is the definitive text:

Cooper, J. (2007). *Cognitive Dissonance: Fifty Years of a Classic Theory.* London: Sage Publications Ltd.

Chapter 5

How judgements influence behaviour

CHAPTER OVERVIEW

Key theories: locus of control, attribution theory, dispositional and situational judgements, covariation model, kinesics and Mehrabian's 7–38–55% rule

5.1 We begin by looking at the theory of locus of control as a mechanism in which to understand how participants judge their own behaviour.

5.2 Next, theories that seek to explain how we judge others are discussed.

5.3 The role of nonverbal communication and making judgements is considered next.

5.4 Finally, the issue of judgement bias and how to mitigate it is discussed.

Introduction

Judgements or attributions as they are referred to in social psychology, are examples of people making sense of everyday actions and it is for this reason that this field of research is sometimes referred to as the psychology of common sense; however, this does a disservice to the importance of attribution in understanding behaviour. Attribution theory deals with how we use information to arrive at causal explanations for behaviour. In other words, we judge by looking to identify and understand the drivers of behaviour. For instance, when we hear a baby cry, we assume it is hungry or upset, whereby we 'attribute' a cause to the crying. The judgements we make about our own behaviour and that of others influence our behaviour, and as such, attribution is a key driver of behaviour.

Why making judgements is important in behavioural research?

Participants make judgements regarding their own behaviour and the behaviour of others.

Researchers make judgements about participant behaviour, including the judgements that participants make about themselves and others. As such, in market research, attribution operates at different levels, as illustrated in Figure 5.1.

As discussed in Section 3.1, much of decision-making is grounded in the unconscious, consequently, individuals can struggle to access the reasons for their behaviour. As we saw earlier, this can result in individuals constructing a reality to make sense of behaviour post hoc. This is also true of making judgements on others, particularly for novel behaviour where individuals have few reference points and, therefore, make judgements to the best of their ability. This can result in poor judgements. Researchers are faced with a unique challenge of making sense of participant judgements about themselves and others, whilst not falling prey to making their own errors of judgement.

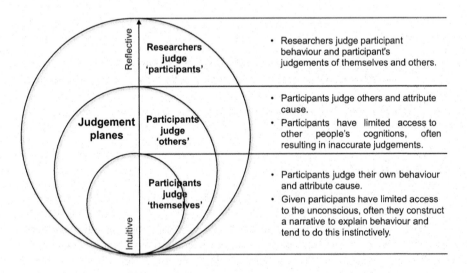

Figure 5.1 Participant and researcher judgements

The extent to which researchers judge participant behaviour is a key area of discussion in social science. Many social scientists assert that analysis should be objective and value-free. Typically, this argument is aligned to an objectivist research philosophy where research observes the laws of experimental science and measures cause and effect. However, objectivist research is not entirely value-free, where researchers choose what subject matter to research and interpret the findings, drawing conclusions that will be influenced by their beliefs and values. It is not possible to conduct an entirely value-free analysis, and inevitably researchers will make judgements about behaviour based on pervading economic, political and cultural influences. Perhaps, the answer to this conundrum is to acknowledge that beliefs and values influence judgements, but the conclusions derived from the research need to be interpreted objectively.

In the beginning

Cause and effect can be traced back to the ancient Greeks. Aristotle suggested there are four causes of behaviour, material, formal, efficient and cause. It is not until the 17th century and the advent of modern philosophy, do we start to see the emergence of the influential work of the philosophers, Hume and Mill. Hume suggested that there are a number of precursors to attribution, not least that causality can only be ascribed as a product of repeated observations. Mill built on this and suggested that we perceive the non-existence of an event as a cause. Mill is considered to be the forefather of contemporary attribution theory.

5.1 Locus of control: making sense of our behaviour

5.1.1 Defining locus of control

It is natural to seek causal explanations for our own behaviour and, as we will see in this chapter, how we explain our behaviour impacts on the likelihood of future behaviour. As we saw earlier, mostly, we do not have access to the unconscious thinking that drove behaviour in the first place; we tend to construct narratives that best fit behaviour. Largely, we are unaware that we are doing it. Further, we post-rationalise behaviour, to reduce cognitive dissonance wherever possible (as discussed in Section 4.5), and again we are mostly unaware we are doing this. In this chapter, we look at the theory of locus of control to help explain how we come to conclusions about our own behaviour and the impact that it has on future behaviour, where locus of control refers to the extent we believe we have control over the outcome of events.

5.1.2 Reviewing locus of control theory

5.1.2.1 Julian B. Rotter's locus of control

The phrase locus of control was first coined by Rotter (1954) and, as noted, refers to the extent to which people believe they have control over the outcome of events in any given situation. Locus of control is often seen as dichotomous, that is, existing in one of two states or orientations, namely, internal or external, as illustrated in Figure 5.2.

For instance, a student might attribute success in their exams to how hard they worked, and this is an internal locus of control. In contrast, another student might attribute the failure in their exams to the examiner not asking the right questions, and this is an external locus of control.

5.1.2.2 Locus of control versus self-efficacy

Self-efficacy was discussed in Section 4.3; one could be forgiven for seeing self-efficacy and locus of control as one and the same; nevertheless, there is a distinction to be made. Self-efficacy refers to an individual's belief in their ability to succeed, in any given situation. Locus of control refers to how much control we believe we have over behavioural outcomes. Naturally, they are causally related, if we feel in control, then our sense of self-efficacy will be higher.

5.1.2.3 Locus of control as a continuum

It is important to acknowledge that whilst locus of control is often presented as a dichotomy, where individuals sit within one of two orientations, this is possibly an oversimplification. Locus of control is more likely a continuum, where participants sit somewhere along the dimension, anchored by internal and external control poles.

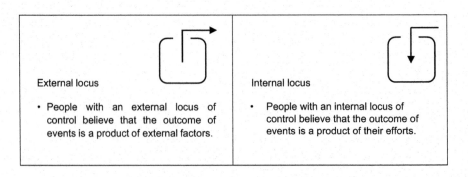

Figure 5.2 Internal and external locus of control

5.1.2.4 Consequences of locus of control

So far, we have considered how attributions are made, within the definition of Rotter's locus of control. Let us now consider the consequences of locus of control on behaviour. Although intuitively one might consider the consequences of an internal orientation to be more favourable to an external, there are pros and cons to each orientation, as illustrated below.

- **Consequences of an internal locus of control:** an individual will be more driven because they feel they have the power to succeed, although this can lead to feelings of inadequacy if they fail at a task.
- **Consequences of an external locus of control:** an individual will be less driven because they feel they do not have the power to succeed, although they might cope better with failure by being able to apportion blame to others. The downside is not being in control might lead to stress and anxiety.

Thus, an internal locus of control is not always better than an external locus of control.

5.1.2.5 Bernard Weiner's attribution theory

Weiner proposed a theory of attribution that seeks to not only explain how we make attributions about our own behaviour but also considers the consequences of attribution. Weiner believed that irrespective of whether we experience a positive or negative outcome, we tend to ask why the outcome has occurred. Weiner and colleagues (1974) built on Rotter's work on locus of control and suggested stability as an additional dimension.

Below, Weiner's dimensions are discussed concerning passing the Market Research Society's diploma in market and social research practise.

Locus of control: as noted, refers to whether an individual attributes behaviour to internal or external factors:

- If one attributes the reason for passing the diploma to hard work, then this is an internal attribution.
- If one attributes failing to pass the diploma to the tutorials not preparing you properly for the exam, then this is an external attribution.

Stability: refers to the extent the cause of an event remains stable over time and in what circumstances:

- If one attributes the reason for passing the diploma to their ability to understand the coursework, then this is a stable attribution.
- If one attributes failing to pass the diploma to not having the time to revise, then this is a less stable attribution.

Later, Weiner added the dimension of controllability to stability and locus of control, as detailed below.

Controllability: refers to the extent to which we feel in control of the causes of behaviour:

- If one attributes the reason for passing the diploma to practising with example questions, then this is entirely controllable behaviour.
- If one attributes failing to pass the diploma to the difficulty of the questions on the day, then this is a non-controllable behaviour.

Using the locus of control, stability and controllable dimensions, it is possible to identify four overarching attribution factors, as illustrated in Figure 5.3.

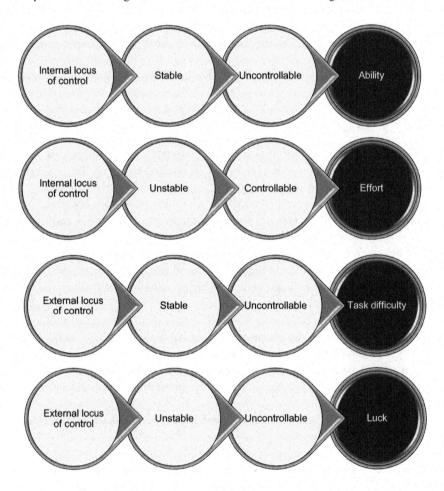

Figure 5.3 Attribution factors

Based on the above attribution factors, we might attribute passing the Market Research Society's diploma in market and social research practise to luck – if we felt that the tutorials had not prepared us properly for the exam (external locus of control), we did not have time to revise (unstable) and felt the questions were overly difficult on the day (uncontrollable).

Our attributions about the outcomes of behaviour will influence future behaviour. Naturally, positive and negative outcomes will encourage or discourage future behaviour, respectively (as seen when we discussed the role of positive and negative conditioning in Section 3.4). Consequently, Weiner's model of attribution is sometimes referred to as a learning or motivational model.

5.1.3 Measuring locus of control in behavioural research

5.1.3.1 Quantitative measurement

There are different question batteries used to measure locus of control. However, the original scale developed by Rotter (1966) is still widely used. The scale consists of a 29-item forced-choice test, including six filler items intended to make the purpose of the test less obvious.

5.1.3.2 Qualitative immersion

In a qualitative setting, the moderator could ask participants to talk about decisions they have made in their life and then look at the factors participants attribute to those events. Further, focusing on locus of control, stability and controllability, will help in understanding the participant's perceptions of the consequences of attribution. Whilst the question areas will be entirely contingent on the research question, the following question areas will help in understanding the nature of locus of control:

- The importance of luck in life.
- The extent to which we feel in control.
- Whether behaviour is on the spur of the moment.
- The importance of a work ethic.
- The extent to which we do what we want to do, rather than what other people expect of us.
- The confidence we have in our opinions.
- The extent to which we defer to others.

5.1.4 Locus of control theory in action

5.1.4.1 Identifying the attitudes towards a cashless society

In this example, locus of control was set against the extent to which consumers were willing to move from using cash to pay for things, to digital alternatives, such

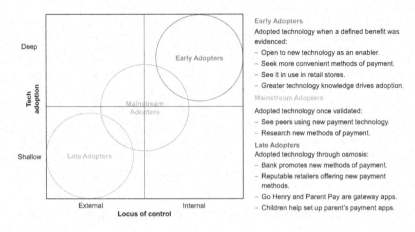

Figure 5.4 Locus of control and cashless payments adoption

as payment apps and contactless. The study was based on 2,000 online consumer interviews. The results are summarised in Figure 5.4.

- Late adopters: exhibit an external locus of control and tend to struggle with the notion of paying for things digitally. Concerns over security abound. With this group, there is a sense of foreboding, a belief that they have little control over the outcome when using digital alternatives; here, technology adoption is at best, by osmosis. To encourage digital payment adoption, this group require considerable hand-holding.
- Mainstream adopters: tend to sit somewhere in the middle of the locus of control orientation, not as self-assured as the early adopters, but more confident than the late adopters. They tend to adopt new forms of technology when it is has been 'tried and tested'.
- Early adopters: exhibit an internal locus of control. They are imbued with confidence which shapes and ultimately defines their behaviour. Digital payment technology adoption is underpinned by a strong sense of self-efficacy.

5.1.4.2 *Measuring reactions to advertising*

Locus of control has been found to be important in understanding reactions to advertising. For example, it has been used to explore women's reactions to advertising where models of different sizes were used in adverts about fattening and non-fattening products (Martin et al., 2007). The study was based on 158 undergraduate female business studies students. Participants were presented with either an advertisement with a larger-sized model or a smaller-sized model. The results were as follows:

- Internal locus of control: participants who believed they could control their weight responded more favourably to smaller models in advertising for non-fattening products.
- External locus of control: participants who felt powerless to control their weight, preferred larger models for non-fattening products.

Interestingly, for fattening products, there is no preference for larger or smaller-sized models. The results from this study suggest that preference for model size is modulated by the participant's perceived ability to control their own weight.

5.1.4.3 Research before purchasing a car

Locus of control has a part to play in what research we do prior to purchasing a car (Srinivasan and Tikoo, 1992). Along with buying a house, a car is one of the most expensive purchases we will make; that said, the extent to which we conduct research prior to purchase varies considerably. Based on a survey of 1401 new car buyers, it was found that the amount of research done prior to purchasing a car is contingent on an individual's locus of control orientation:

- Internal locus of control: consumers conducted research into what was the most suitable car, spent longer time researching cars, considered more models, visited a greater number of dealerships and test drove more cars. All this helped to rationalise the final car purchase decision.
- External locus of control: consumers did very little research, considered fewer cars, visited fewer dealerships and test drove fewer cars. It was argued that the car purchasing experience was already stressful enough and that conducting extensive research prior to purchase only served to make the process more confusing.

The results from this study suggest that those with an internal locus of control, look at ways in which to inform and control decision-making, whereas the opposite is true for external locus of control, where such efforts are seen to confound decision-making.

5.1.4.4 Identifying small business international trading ambitions

Locus of control can be applied to business decision-making. In the example below, locus of control was used to predict businesses' ambition to trade internationally. A total of 500 small to medium-sized businesses completed an online survey. To measure locus of control, participants were presented with the following statements and asked to indicate the extent they agreed with each on a five-point agreement scale.

Statements:

- In business a certain degree of luck is required.
- We feel that many competitor businesses are better placed to deal with current market conditions.
- We tend not to plan formally but respond to market events as and when they happen.
- The success of our business is a product of careful strategic planning.
- We feel confident that when we make plans, we can realise them.

The cohorts detailed in Figure 5.5, were identified using k-means cluster analysis (a statistical technique used to find groups of individuals with a similar profile/needs) and then profiled.

As can be seen, by placing businesses on the locus of control dimension, we can identify clearly defined groups of businesses which, when profiled, exhibit distinct and mutually exclusive intentions and behavioural traits regarding international trade:

- Internal locus of control: tended to be growing, aspirant businesses, who were in control and who had planned for international expansion.

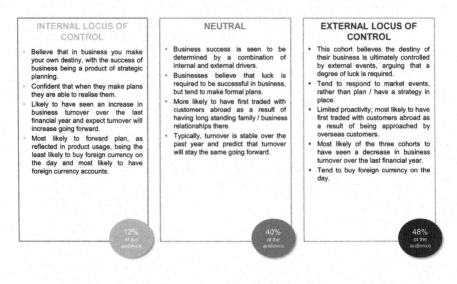

Figure 5.5 Locus of control and business ambitions

- Neutral: sitting in between the internal and external poles, typically, stable businesses, where some had made plans for international expansion but had not necessarily executed them.
- External locus of control: some businesses had witnessed negative growth. These businesses tended to react to market changes and as such, were not necessarily in control; typically, those that had traded abroad had done so only when approached by an existing overseas customer.

5.1.4.5 Attribution and employee promotion

Daly (1998) looked at career development amongst government employees in America. Attribution theory was used to examine the causal explanations government employees gave for not being promoted or not being given developmental opportunities. The sample was composed of those that had applied for but had been denied a promotion or a developmental opportunity over a period of five years. It was found that mostly the reasons for promotion denial were attributed to factors that were uncontrollable:

- Uncontrollable/unstable attributions: the most cited attribution related to the existence of an 'old boys' network, where members of the in-group do favours for each other.
- Uncontrollable/stable attributions: age, race and gender bias were cited as reasons for promotion denial.

Although this study is based on perceptions, the findings are concerning, suggesting that promotion is less about merit and more about factors that employees have little control over.

5.1.4.6 Individual differences

There are key differences by age, gender, socio-economic class and culture. Longitudinal studies suggest that up to the mid-40s, our internal locus control increases and begins to wane thereafter. A study of 7,500 British adults demonstrated that an internal locus of control at the age of ten reduces the chances of obesity at the age of 30 (Gale et al., 2008). On balance, females tend to load more on an external locus of control as compared to their male counterparts. Children whose parents have an external locus of control are more likely to attribute their successes and failures to external causes. Further, people that come from lower socio-economic backgrounds, tend to exhibit an external locus of control. When comparing people in Japan to those in America, it seems that the Japanese exhibit a more external locus of control, than Americans. As noted earlier, this might reflect differences in collective versus individualistic societies.

5.1.5 Implications for behavioural research

1   In making sense of our own behaviour, we tend to attribute behaviour to internal and external factors. As such, an understanding of locus of control is important in market research.
2   Locus of control is often seen as a dichotomy, existing in one of the two states, however, it is better understood as a continuum, where people sit somewhere on the dimension, as illustrated by the examples presented in this chapter.
3   Attribution theory suggests that to understand behaviour we need to look at the consequences of behaviour and look not only at locus of control but stability and controllability. Understanding the consequence of behaviour is important because it is a predictor of future behaviour.
4   When measuring locus of control, it is important to develop questions that are specific to the research question under inspection. There are numerous scales to select questions from, along with those detailed in this chapter. In a qualitative setting, researchers should explore different behavioural outcomes and probe how participants have attributed these experiences.

5.1.6 References/further reading

Daly, D. (1998). Attribution Theory and the Glass Ceiling: Career Development among Federal Employees. *International Journal of Organisational Theory and Research*, 1 (1), pp. 93–116.

Gale, C., Batty, D., and Deary, I. (2008). Locus of Control at Age 10 Years and Health Outcomes and Behaviors at Age 30 Years: The 1970 British Cohort Study. *Psychosomatic Medicine*, 70 (4), pp. 397–403.

Martin, B., Veer, E., and Pervan, S. (2007). Self-Referencing and Consumer Evaluations of Larger-Sized Female Models: A Weight Locus of Control Perspective. *Marketing Letters*. 18 (3), pp. 197–209.

Rotter, J. B. (1954). *Social Learning and Clinical Psychology*. Englewood Cliffs, NJ: Prentice-Hall.

Rotter, J. B. (1966). Generalized Expectancies for Internal Versus External Control of Reinforcement. *Psychological Monographs: General and Applied*, 80, pp. 1–28.

Srinivasan, N., and Tikoo, S. (1992). *Effect of Locus of Control on Information Search Behavior*, in NA – Advances in Consumer Research Volume 19, eds. John F. Sherry, Jr. and Brian Sternthal, Provo, UT: Association for Consumer Research, pp. 498–504.

Weiner, B. (1974). *Achievement Motivation and Attribution Theory*. Morristown, N.J.: General Learning Press.

5.1.6.1 Want to know more?

Most psychology textbooks on personality or individual differences will address locus of control. There are books that specifically look at locus of control, but they tend to be from the self-help/empowerment genre, typically looking at ways in which to encourage an internal locus of control, for our purposes, such books offer the reader limited value.

5.2 Judging others: making sense of other people's behaviour

5.2.1 Defining attributions about other people's behaviour

Not only do we make judgements about our own behaviour but we judge others. It is second nature to make judgements about other people's behaviour. Judging others helps us make sense of the social world. As with attribution and our own behaviour, understanding why people behave the way they do gives us a sense of control, which in turn influences our behaviour. There are several theories that look at the attribution of other people's behaviour; we start by reviewing Heider's distinction between dispositional and situational attributions and then look at Jones and Davis' research exploring the link between attribution and intentions before finally looking at Kelly's covariation model of attribution.

5.2.2 Reviewing attribution theory

5.2.2.1 Fritz Heider's dispositional and situational judgements

Heider suggested that we are naïve psychologists trying to make sense of human behaviour (Heider, 1958). Heider believed that we observe, analyse and then attempt to explain behaviour by attributing behaviour to either dispositional or situational factors that lead to internal or external attributions, respectively, as detailed in Figure 5.6.

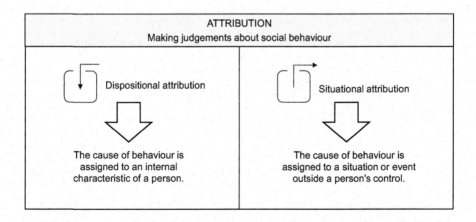

Figure 5.6 Dispositional and situational factors and attribution

As naïve psychologists, we look at behaviour in terms of ability, which is assumed to be relatively stable and motivation, which is assumed to be variable. There is thought to be an interrelationship between ability, motivation and behaviour. If there is limited ability then the behaviour will be unlikely; similarly, with limited motivation, behaviour will be unlikely. Some ability and motivation will greatly increase the likelihood of behaviour. We make inferences, based on what we know. If we know the behavioural outcome and we have some sense of the motivation behind the behaviour, we can make a judgement in terms of ability.

For example, take two cyclists on a time trial, during the trial they achieve the same time. One trained long and hard and the other just turned up on the day; we can assume that the cyclist who did not train demonstrated greater ability. Similarly, we can make assumptions about a cyclist's effort if we know about the ability and the difficulty of the task. If the two cyclists achieve different times on the same time trial but had similar abilities, then we could assume that one cyclist put in more effort than the other.

5.2.2.2 Edward Jones and Keith Davis' correspondent inference theory

Jones and Davis (1965) sought to understand how we make dispositional attributions (attribution based on internal characteristics of an individual). Like Heider, Jones and Davis looked at the process that allows us to make inferences based on observed behaviour. It is thought that we tend to make dispositional attributions when we see a 'correspondence' between intentions and actual behaviour. The correspondent inference theory describes the conditions under which we make dispositional attributions. To infer intentions from behaviour, there has to be a certain degree of knowledge about the behaviour in the first place. Jones and Davis identified factors that increase the likelihood of correspondence inferences and, consequently, a dispositional attribution, as illustrated in Table 5.1.

5.2.2.3 Harold Kelly's covariation model

Like Heider, Kelly (1967) argued that when trying to attribute causes of behaviour we behave much like scientists; we consider the available evidence over time, whether that be something about the person or the circumstance or a combination of these factors and we then draw conclusions and make attributions. According to Kelly's theory, we do this by taking into consideration three categories of evidence, as illustrated in Table 5.2.

Table 5.1 Factors in correspondence inferences

Factors	Definition	Example
Choice	If a behaviour is freely chosen it is believed to be a product of some internal aspect of the person.	If an individual chooses to vote for the Green Party in the local elections, we can infer that the person's actions reflect some internally held political or environmental view.
Social desirability	Low levels of social desirability are thought to suggest behaviour is a product of some internal aspect of the individual.	If a nurse is kind and considerate to a patient, we infer that this is indicative of the role of a nurse. Alternatively, if a nurse is rude and abrasive to a patient, then we infer that this is because of the nurse's mood or character.
Personalism	If an individual's behaviour appears to be intended to have an impact on others, we assume that it is 'personal', and not just a consequence of the situation.	If someone parks too close to us on the road, we infer that this action is to deliberately box us in, rather than because there was nowhere else to park, or because it was an oversight by the motorist.
Hedonistic relevance	If an individual's behaviour appears to be directly intended to cause harm or be beneficial to the individual, it is assumed to be a result of an internal aspect of the person.	If, at a party, a guest takes two slices of cake, then we assume they are greedy and selfish, what we might not know is they intend to share the second slice with another party guest.
Non-common effects	The extent to which the effects on behaviour are different from one action to another. It is assumed that, if the effects across different behaviours are different (i.e. non-common), then the chances of a dispositional inference are high.	When looking for a new car, if one chooses a BMW 3 Series over a BMW 5 Series, it is difficult to make inferences about someone's disposition. However, if one chooses, a Skoda Yeti over a BMW 3 Series, then there is sufficient difference for us to infer dispositional aspects.
Expectancies: Category-based	Derived from our knowledge about particular types or groups of people.	You frequent a casino and sitting at the roulette table is a person with a clerical collar, you assume that an individual of the cloth would not condone gambling and infer that their behaviour is a product of something internal about them.
Expectancies: Target-based	Derived from knowledge about a particular person.	Finding out that a person is a supporter of Donald Trump sets up a number of expectations about their political views and beliefs.

Table 5.2 Covariation model

Influencers	Definition
Consensus	• The extent to which other people behave the same way in a similar situation.
Distinctiveness	• The extent to which a person behaves the same way in a similar situation.
Consistency	• The extent to which a person behaves the same way in the same situation.

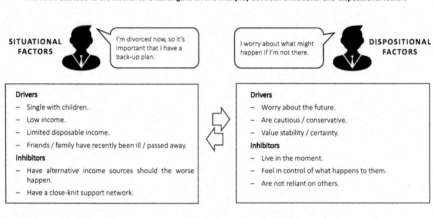

The value ascribed to life insurance is contingent on the interplay between situational and dispositional factors

Figure 5.7 Dispositional and situational factors in life insurance purchase

5.2.3 Attribution theory in action

5.2.3.1 Dispositional and situational influences

Considering dispositional and situational factors is a simple but effective framework in which to understand drivers to behaviour. In this example, research was commissioned to understand the drivers of purchasing life insurance. In-depth interviews were conducted amongst consumers from a broad range of life stages. It was found that drivers and inhibitors to purchasing life insurance were a result of an interplay between dispositional and situational, as illustrated in Figure 5.7.

5.2.3.2 Covariation factors and everyday decision-making

In Figure 5.8, we look at an example of covariation and attribution when buying a sandwich from Pret a Manger for lunch at work.

Consensus	Distinctiveness	Consistency
• If Johnnie buys a sandwich from Pret and other work colleagues also buy a sandwich from Pret, then we have a high consensus. Johnnie's behaviour is attributable to situational factors.	• If Johnnie only buys sandwiches from Pret when at work, then Johnnie's behaviour is distinctive and so his behaviour is attributable to situational factors.	• If Johnnie buys sandwiches from Pret every working day, then we have high consistency and so Johnnie's behaviour is attributable to situational factors.
• If no other work colleagues buy sandwiches from Pret, then we have a low consensus and Johnnie's behaviour is attributable to dispositional factors.	• If Johnnie buys sandwiches from Pret at work and at home, then distinctiveness is low and Johnnie's behaviour is attributable to dispositional factors.	• If Johnnie buys sandwiches from Pret every now and then, then we have low consistency and Johnnie's behaviour is attributed to dispositional factors.

Figure 5.8 Dispositional and situational factors and buying a sandwich

5.2.4 *Implications for behavioural research*

1   Individuals make judgements about other people's behaviour. Mostly, they are not privy to all the factors at play and, consequently, such judgements are based on incomplete knowledge. Attribution theory provides researchers with a framework in which we understand how participants go about filling in the blanks.

2   Dispositional and situational attribution provides researchers with a simple but effective way in which to explain and predict participant behaviour.

3   Attribution theory is applicable to behaviour in most social settings. Thus, attribution is at the very heart of behavioural research.

4   Market researchers observe and listen and make judgements, and in so doing, they make dispositional and situational attributions.

5.2.5 *References/further reading*

Heider, F. (1958; reprint, 2015). *The Psychology of Interpersonal Relations*. Eastford: Martino Fine Books.

Jones, E. E., and Davis, K. E. (1965). From Acts to Dispositions: The Attribution Process in Social Psychology. In L. Berkowitz (Ed.), *Advances in Experimental Social Psychology*, 2, pp. 219–266. New York: Academic Press.

Kelley, H. H. (1967). Attribution Theory in Social Psychology. In D. Levine (Ed.), *Nebraska Symposium on Motivation*, 15, pp. 192–238. Lincoln: University of Nebraska Press.

5.2.5.1 Want to know more?

Försterling's book provides a good overall grounding in attribution theory and its application:
Försterling, F. (2001). *Attribution: An Introduction to Theories, Research and Applications.* East Sussex: Psychology Press Ltd.

5.3 Nonverbal communication: how to read nonverbal cues

5.3.1 *Defining nonverbal communication*

In the previous chapter, we discussed how individuals make attributions. In this chapter, we look at the role of nonverbal communication and attribution. Nonverbal communication is the use of physical behaviour, expressions and mannerisms to communicate nonverbally. Intriguingly, nonverbal communication is instinctive, it is driven by the unconscious and is automatic in nature. That is, we are largely unaware we are communicating nonverbally. Given this, it is difficult to lie nonverbally. However, it would be wrong to assume all communication is driven by the unconscious mind. Take smiling for instance; it can be a genuine and natural reaction when we are pleased to meet with someone, or it can be forced and controlled when we are less than pleased to meet someone.

We are continuously giving and receiving wordless signals. Even when we are silent, we are still communicating, just nonverbally, whether that be the gestures we make, the way we sit, how close we stand to one another, whether there is eye contact or not and so on. Each day we make and receive thousands of nonverbal messages. For instance, someone who is self-conscious about their weight might smooth down their clothing, and someone who is nervous before a job interview might tug at their skin under their chin or might cross their arms or legs as a defensive mechanism. As such, nonverbal communication is an outward expression of an individual's emotional state of mind.

Whilst there is some debate around exactly how much of our communication is nonverbal, a typical figure cited is 70%, leaving only 30% accounted for verbal communication. By any measure, 70% is significant. Naturally, participants judge the nonverbal communication of others and researchers judge the nonverbal communication of participants. Take, for instance, a focus group, not all the communication between participants and moderator is verbal, mostly they are communicating nonverbally. Participants are making judgements about other participants and the moderator based on nonverbal communication. Also, the moderator is making judgements about the participants based on their nonverbal communication. For observation research, we are not at liberty to hear or engage verbally with the subject, and as such, we are entirely reliant on nonverbal cues.

Given the significance of nonverbal cues in communication, it is important that researchers are able to read this type of communication in order to attribute behaviour accurately. In this chapter, the different forms of nonverbal communication are discussed. We start by looking at Birdwhistell's theory of kinesics, which was the first formative theory of nonverbal communication and Mehrabian's rule on nonverbal communication, before looking at specific examples of nonverbal communication.

5.3.2 Reviewing nonverbal communication theory

5.3.2.1 Ray Birdwhistell's kinesics

Curiously, the study of nonverbal communication only gained momentum in the 1960s and has since become a subject of interest in anthropology, sociology, psychology, psychiatry and further afield. In the 1950s, the anthropologist, Birdwhistell was the first to systematically study nonverbal communication. He founded kinesics, the study of body motion and nonverbal aspects of interpersonal communication (Birdwhistell, 1952).

Birdwhistell drew on the principles of linguistics, arguing that like language, body language has a grammar of its own that can be analysed in a way similar to verbal communications. He filmed people in different social settings and analysed the recordings, looking at posture, gestures and movement (previously, the study of body movements had been based on still photos). Like phonemes in linguistics, Birdwhistell referred to groups of movements as kinemes. Birdwhistell believed that all communication is a product of socialisation and as such, the meaning of different nonverbal cues varies according to different cultures; this led him to conclude that body movements are not universal. Contemporary researchers have come to challenge this notion. For instance, we now know that facial expressions are universal, that is, they exist irrespective of culture. Notwithstanding this obvious flaw in Birdwhistesll's theorising, kinesics put nonverbal communication on the research map and stimulated considerable interest in the field of nonverbal communication, which continues to this day.

5.3.2.2 Albert Mehrabian's 7-38–55% rule

In the 1960s, Mehrabian was interested in nonverbal communication and face-to-face exchanges and conducted a couple of pioneering studies into nonverbal communication. The first study looked at inconsistencies between the meaning conveyed by the spoken word and nonverbal cues (Mehrabian and Wiener, 1967). Participants were asked to listen to voices repeatedly saying 'maybe' in different tones of voice to convey three emotional states, such as like, dislike or neutrality. At the same time, participants were shown pictures of people attempting to express each of the emotional states. The results of this study led Mehrabian to conclude that facial expression was a better indication of an emotional state than the spoken word.

Building on this study, Mehrabian looked at participants' ability to discern emotional states using the spoken word and the tone of voice (Mehrabian and Ferris, 1967). In this study, participants were asked to listen to words that attempted to convey liking (positive language), disliking (negative language) or neutrality (neutral language). Each word was spoken with a different tone of voice. Participants were randomly assigned to one of three groups.

- Group 1: were instructed to ignore the meaning of the word and focus on tone of voice.
- Group 2: were instructed to focus on the meaning of the word and ignore the tone of voice.
- Group 3: were instructed to focus on both the meaning of the word and the tone of voice.

The results from this study led Mehrabian to conclude that tone of voice was a stronger indicator of an emotional state than the meaning of the word. Based on both studies, Mehrabian put forward the 7–38–55% rule, where liking communication is accounted for by 7% spoken words, 38% tone of voice and 55% body language. There is some debate about the robustness of the experimental design of both studies, not least that it is difficult to objectively measure tone of voice and body language. There are also issues of ecological validity, where strictly speaking the rule applies to liking as an emotion. Indeed, Mehrabian's rule has been mispresented and applied more widely to all forms of communication. Nonetheless, Mehrabian's work unequivocally demonstrates the significance of nonverbal communications in reading different emotional states.

5.3.2.3 *Nature versus nurture debate*

There is much debate about the extent to which nonverbal communication is a product of socialisation or biology. As is often the case with the nature versus nurture debate, the answer is nuanced:

- Nature: smiling expressions in children born deaf and blind occur in absence of learning or imitating. Studies into facial expressions from different cultures suggest that humans tend to use the same basic facial expressions to demonstrate emotion. Interestingly, higher-order primates have a similar range of facial expressions to humans. This would suggest some innate traits to nonverbal communication, at least for facial expressions.
- Nurture: when a baby has had enough milk, it turns its head from side to side, and when the toddler has had enough to eat, it shakes its head from

side to side; the child learns to use this form of nonverbal communication as it grows up. Gestures and expressions can mean different things in different cultures. This would suggest some learned behaviour, at least for gestures and expressions.

In practice, nonverbal communication is a product of both innate traits and behaviour learned during socialisation. Further, it could be argued that we have an innate ability to learn nonverbal communication.

5.3.2.4 The role of nonverbal communication

If we are to understand nonverbal communication, we must first consider the purpose of this form of communication. The consensus is for five core functions of nonverbal communication, as illustrated in Table 5.3.

5.3.3 Identifying different types of nonverbal communication

As illustrated in Figure 5.9, it is surprising just how many different forms of nonverbal communication there are.

In reading participants, it is important to be cognisant of all forms of nonverbal communication. Naturally, in certain situations, some nonverbal cues will be more important than others. Below, the various forms of nonverbal communication are presented.

Table 5.3 Core functions of nonverbal communication

Function	Definition
Substitution	• To fill in for verbal communication, such as, shaking our head rather than saying no, or waving when saying goodbye.
Accentuation	• To accent the meaning of verbal messages, such as, pointing whilst conveying directions.
Complement	• To reinforce verbal communication, such as, indicating sarcasm by the tone of voice or rubbing one's stomach when indicating hunger.
Contradiction	• To contradict a verbal cue such as, saying yes when someone asks you if you are okay, but then rolling your eyes or hunching your shoulders.
Regulation	• To regulate the flow of communication, such as nodding when in agreement; gaining eye contact might suggest you have something to add, whilst closed lips are an indication of nothing else to add.

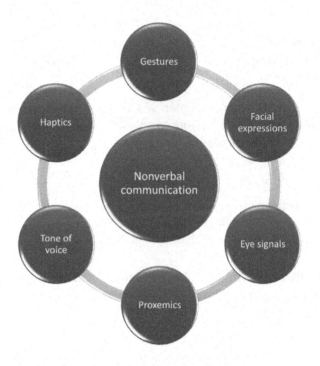

Figure 5.9 Different forms of nonverbal communication

5.3.3.1 Gestures

In Table 5.4, some of the more obvious examples of gestures are presented.

5.3.3.2 Facial expressions

A facial expression is one or more motions or positions of the muscles beneath the skin of the face. There are over 40 muscles in the face that can make thousands of combinations. These movements convey the emotional state of an individual.

The American TV show 'Lie to Me' aired between 2009 and 2011. In the show, Cal Lightman was a leading expert in the study of facial expressions and body language; he helped local and federal police solve crimes by observing micro facial expressions and body language to uncover the truth. The character was loosely based on Paul Ekman, the renowned psychologist and specialist in facial expressions and emotions. Although fictional, the show demonstrated how relatively subtle changes in facial expression can be powerful nonverbal signals. There are broadly six core facial expressions, as detailed in Table 5.5.

Table 5.4 Universal gestures

Gesture	Definition
Rubbing hands together	• To convey positive expectation.
Head nod	• To denote a yes.
Head tilt	• To suggest submission/the neck and throat are less threatening.
Head down	• To show disapproval or dejection.
Hands clenched together	• To show restraint and anxious state of mind.
The steeple	• To demonstrate confidence/self-assured attitudes; can be seen as an expression of superiority.
Thumbs up	• To indicate confidence and authority.
Waving	• To express a greeting.
Legs spread apart	• To demonstrate confidence, almost entirely a male gesture.
The starter position	• To indicate a readiness to engage, including sitting down, leaning forward and hands on knees.
Show of palms	• To demonstrate openness, typically an unconscious gesture.

Table 5.5 Facial expressions

Expression	Definition
Disgust	• Upper nose wrinkle and upper lip raised.
Sadness	• Drooping under eyelids, losing focus in eyes and slight pulling down of lip corners.
Anger	• Eyebrows down together, eye glare and narrowing of lips.
Contempt	• Lip corner tightening and raised on one side of the face.
Surprise	• Eyebrows raised, eyes widened and mouth open.
Fear	• Eyebrows raised and pulled together.

5.3.3.3 Eye signals

We are all familiar with the phrase 'the eyes are the window to the soul', but to what extent is this true? Eye signals are an important form of nonverbal communication. The eyes convey a broad spectrum of emotions including, interest, affection, attraction and hostility. Eye contact is also important in maintaining the

Gaze	Blinking
– Holding one's gaze indicates honesty. – Inability to maintain gaze is frequently seen as an indicator of someone who is lying / being deceptive.	– Increased blinking is an indication of interest. – Blinking can also be a product of stress. – A single blink can indicate surprise.
Dilation	Eyebrows
– When people light on things they like, there is a tendency for the pupils to dilate. – Pupils dilation is also associated with anger / negative mood.	– The eyebrow raise indicates surprise or disapproval and is an unconscious gesture.

Figure 5.10 Eye signals

flow of conversation and for gauging other people's interests and responses. The four key eye signals are detailed in Figure 5.10.

5.3.3.4 Proxemics 'proximity'

Proxemics refers to our personal space and as such is an important form of non-verbal communication. The amount of distance we feel comfortable with is influenced by a number of factors that we discussed in previous chapters including social norms, personality and familiarity. Distances that we are comfortable with also depend on the situational factors at play. Although there is some debate about the exact distance for different situations, the distances detailed in Figure 5.11 are typically cited.

5.3.3.5 Tone of voice 'paralinguistics'

Paralinguistics is the study of nonverbal cues of the voice and includes timing and cadence, how loud one speaks, tone, inflexion and sounds that convey understanding, such as "ahh" and "uh-huh". Tone of voice can indicate sarcasm, anger, affection or confidence. In Figure 5.12, the typical forms of paralinguistic communication are detailed.

A change in tone of voice can change the meaning of a sentence. A friend might ask you how you are doing and you might answer "I'm fine", but how you

The four broad categories of space

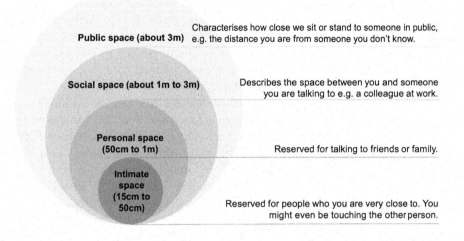

Figure 5.11 Distances by category

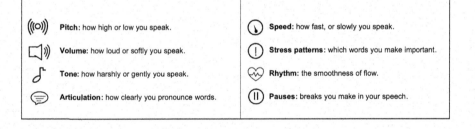

Figure 5.12 Tone of voice

actually say those words can reveal a tremendous amount. A bright, happy tone of voice will reveal that you are doing okay. A sombre, downcast tone would indicate that you are not fine. A cold tone of voice might suggest that actually, you are not fine, but you do not wish to discuss it.

5.3.3.6 Haptics 'touch'

Communicating through touch is another important nonverbal behaviour. The word haptics comes from the Greek word *haptikos*, which means to touch. Touch can communicate a vast array of different emotions including, affection, trust and sympathy. If we take the humble handshake as an example, we can begin to appreciate the infinite power of touch. Handshakes are a remnant of the past. It is thought that the handshake dates back to ancient Greece (depiction of two soldiers shaking hands can be found on part of a 5th century BC funerary stele on display in the Pergamon Museum, Berlin). The handshake was used to demonstrate that neither party was carrying a weapon. The lower arm greeting by Romans was an extension of this. In the 19th century, the handshake was used to seal a transaction; today, we use it in business and increasingly in social settings.

There is an infinite range of different meanings to touch. As such, making sense of touch is challenging. For instance, a hug suggests intimacy and comfort. A pat on the back or rubbing someone's arm suggests sympathy. Gripping of the arm suggests security or support. An arm around someone's shoulder would suggest protectiveness. Of course, many of these forms of touch have more than one meaning, so they should be interpreted within the context of the situation. For example, gripping of the arm could also indicate control. On occasion, touch is accidental. As such, be sure to evaluate this form of nonverbal communication in combination with other nonverbal and verbal communication at that moment.

5.3.3.7 Mirroring

We imitate the nonverbal behaviour of others and this is called mirroring. It is thought to improve rapport. In physical mirroring, we imitate the posture and mannerisms of others. We also mirror proximity, where there is an ongoing negotiation as one person moves out and the other moves in until a distance that both parties are comfortable with is achieved.

5.3.3.8 Individual differences

Children are easier to read than adults, they are more expressive facially and are less likely to have learnt the art of deception. When a child tells a lie, it is not uncommon for the child to spontaneously put a hand over their mouth. As teenagers, we tend to rub our fingers lightly over our mouths when we lie. As adults, we tend to place our hands near to our mouth, but typically at the last moment, we touch our nose. It seems age brings a degree of sophistication (not self-evident as a child) and subtly to our gestures which inevitably makes the task of reading more difficult.

There are many cultural differences in nonverbal communications, including:

■ In India, the head-rocking from side to side indicates yes, whilst in Arab countries, using a single up head movement means no.
■ Italians tend to be more expressive when they are excited than other nationalities.

- Making a circle with your thumb and forefinger means ok in western cultures, in Japan, this sign refers to money.
- Countries that are densely populated generally have much less need for personal space than those that are not. For instance, the Japanese are less likely to react strongly to an accidental touch by a stranger, than Americans.
- In America, hands on hips indicates power and pride, but in Argentina, it is considered an expression of anger.
- In Colombia, Argentina, Chile and Peru, one kiss is considered an acceptable form of greeting. In Spain, Greece and Italy, two kisses are the norm. In Belgium, Slovenia, Macedonia and Serbia, it is three kisses.
- Mostly, when greeting someone, hands are shaken four or five times, in Germany, it is customary to shake hands only twice.

5.3.4 Measuring nonverbal communication in behavioural research

5.3.4.1 Cold reading

When engaged in any form of qualitative research, whether that be one-to-one interviews, focus groups or observational research, we need to be able to judge nonverbal communication and make attributions. Perhaps one of the more obvious examples of making sense of nonverbal communication is cold reading. Cold reading is based on careful observation of body language, where the 'reader' decodes a person's reactions to questions. This is a common technique amongst tarot card readers, psychics, astrologists and palm readers who present the illusion of clairvoyant power. Tarot cards, together with the mystical physical setting, can convince even the most hardened sceptic of the efficacy of cold reading. Intriguingly, many are so good at cold reading that they genuinely believe that they have a gift, which adds to the authenticity of the experience.

5.3.4.2 Rules of interpretation

In absence of any mystical power, researchers can apply the rules detailed in Figure 5.13.

The rules are not mutually exclusive, it is important to be mindful of all rules when observing and judging nonverbal communication. Observing these rules will help to minimise attribution errors. To help 'read' nonverbal communication watch a video recording of a focus group or a one-to-one interview with the sound turned down, attempt to read the nonverbal cues of the participants, then listen back to the recording and use the verbal communication to consensus check your nonverbal read.

Look for
congruence

- Avoid reading too much into a single gesture or nonverbal cue.
- Consider all the nonverbal signals available, from eye contact to tone of voice and so on.

Look for
consistency

- Look for consistencies between verbal and nonverbal communication.
- Nonverbal communication should reinforce what is being said, not contradict it. Is the person saying one thing, but their body language conveying something else?

Look for
situational factors

- Situational factors help to contextual nonverbal communication. For instance, a limp handshake is often thought to suggest weakness in a man. What if they are an artist or musician? They might prefer not to shake hands and if they must, only tentatively.

Figure 5.13 Rules of interpretation

5.3.5 Implications for behavioural research

1 Nonverbal communication accounts for up to 70% of our communication and as such, judging nonverbal cues is a key part of making sense of participant behaviour.
2 Much of the nonverbal communication we see when in focus groups, one-to-one interviews and observational research is relatively instinctive and spontaneous in nature and, as such, participants are mostly unaware of their nonverbal communication.
3 Earlier in this chapter a distinction between dispositional and situational factors was made; observing and making sense of nonverbal communication helps in distinguishing between dispositional and situational factors.
4 In behavioural research, we process a vast array of nonverbal cues and trying to make sense of it is challenging. In interpreting this data, we should be mindful of congruence, consistency and situational context.

5.3.6 References/further reading

Birdwhistell, R. L. (1952). *Introduction to Kinesics: An Annotation System for Analysis of Body Motion and Gesture.* Washington, DC: Department of State, Foreign Service Institute.

Mehrabian, A., and Ferris, S. R. (1967). Inference of Attitudes from Nonverbal Communication in Two Channels. *Journal of Consulting Psychology*, 31 (3), pp. 248–252.

Mehrabian, A., and Wiener, M. (1967). Decoding of Inconsistent Communications. *Journal of Personality and Social Psychology*, 6 (1), pp. 109–114.

5.3.6.1 Want to know more?

If you wish to learn more about kinesics, then Birdwhistell's book *Kinesics and Context* is a synthesis of over two decades of work.

Birdwhistell, R. (1970). *Kinesics and Context: Essays on Body Motion Communication.* Philadelphia: University of Pennsylvania Press.

For a more general introduction to nonverbal communication then the following book is a good place to start:

Pease, A., and Pease, B. (2017). *The Definitive Book of Body Language.* London: Orion Books.

For a critical discussion about the face and emotions then the following is recommended:

Ekman, P. (2015). *Emotion in the Human Face.* San Jose: Malor Books.

5.4 Making judgements in practice: controlling for bias

5.4.1 Defining judgement bias

So far, we have looked at attribution theory in terms of judging our own behaviour and that of others. Mostly, these theories assume that people are amateur social scientists, formulating hypotheses, weighing the evidence and ascribing cause and affect accordingly. In reality, the process of attribution is problematic. Whilst judging our own behaviour, we struggle to recall why we did what we did and attempt to construct fiction to make sense of this. When judging others, we are often not in receipt of all the information to make an informed decision. Unsurprisingly, attribution mistakes or biases are common. In the final part of this chapter, we look at some of the more obvious biases when judging our own behaviour and that of others.

5.4.2 Judgement bias about our own behaviour

Let us start by considering the key judgement biases made when judging our own behaviour, as illustrated in Table 5.6.

Table 5.6 Judgement biases about our own behaviour

Bias	Definition
Self-serving bias	• Attributing success to dispositional factors and failure to situational factors. • It is thought to be a defence mechanism to guard against having to take responsibility for failure which could potentially have an adverse effect on self-esteem.
False-consensus bias	• The assumption that our attitudes and behaviours are shared by others. • It is thought to be motivational, whereby we assume that our behaviour is normative and consequently attribute it to others. • This bias is common in group settings, where a person might think that the collective views, opinions and behaviours of that group are broadly similar to the wider population (as we saw with groupthink in Section 2.4).

5.4.3 Judgement bias about others' behaviour

Next, biases in judgements about other people's behaviour are presented in Table 5.7.

5.4.4 Judgement biases in action

Let us now look at some examples of judgement biases.

5.4.4.1 Judgement bias and our own behaviour

5.4.4.1.1 SELF-SERVING BIAS: INTERPERSONAL RELATIONSHIPS

Sedikides et al. (1998) were concerned with interpersonal relationships and self-serving bias. Close and distant relationship partners were asked to complete a task. When distant partners worked on the task together, they tended to take credit for success but attributed failure to their partner. Close partners did not take more credit than their partner for success and did not blame their partner more than themselves for failure. In other words, close couples did not exhibit a self-serving bias. The researchers surmised that the lack of self-serving bias was because of a favourable impression of the partner, which, in turn, reduced the need for self-enhancing tendencies.

5.4.4.1.2 FALSE-CONSENSUS BIAS: COLLEGE STUDENTS AND PEER-GROUP IDENTITY

Bauman and Geher (2002) were interested in the effects of false-consensus bias amongst college students. College students were asked to complete a questionnaire

Table 5.7 Judgement biases about other people's behaviour

Bias	Definition
Fundamental attribution error	• There is a tendency to attribute other people's behaviour largely to dispositional factors. • This reflects a predisposition to underestimate how important the social situation is in determining behaviour. • We are not privy to the consistency and distinctiveness of that behaviour and base attribution almost entirely on consensus information, often leading to a dispositional attribution. • This type of bias can lead to prejudice and stereotyping.
Just world bias	• There is a tendency to make attribution errors based on a belief that the world is fundamentally just and fair. • We look for ways to explain injustices by ascribing causality to dispositional factors of the victim.
Availability bias (or availability heuristic)	• We make judgements based on how easily related events or situations come to mind. • If we can easily recall events or situations, we assume that these events or situations are more prevalent than might be the case.
Beauty is good bias	• The adage 'don't judge a book by its cover' does not seem to play out in reality. • Physical characteristics play an important role in how we judge people. For example, those that are considered physically attractive are seen to have attractive personalities.
'In-' and 'out-' group bias	• We tend to attribute the behaviour of a group that we identify with to dispositional factors and the behaviour of a group we do not identify with to situational factors.

on a variety of social topics where they were asked to state how they felt about each subject and the extent to which they thought others shared their views. The findings suggested that most of the social subjects discussed resulted in a false-consensus bias, particularly when students were referencing fellow students. In other words, it was assumed that their views on social subjects were shared by their immediate peer group.

5.4.4.2 *Judgement bias and other people's behaviour*

5.4.4.2.1 FUNDAMENTAL ATTRIBUTION ERROR: PERCEPTIONS OF
      INTELLIGENCE

In Skitka et al's (2002) experiment, subjects were read a story about a trivia quiz, where volunteers were randomly assigned to quizmaster and participant roles.

The quizmaster was instructed to come up with five questions to which they knew the answer and then put the questions to the participant. The participant was able to answer only one of the questions correctly. The subjects were then asked to comment on the intelligence of both the quizmaster and the participant. Intriguingly, the quizmaster was seen to be smarter than the participant, even though the participant was clearly at a disadvantage, where the quizmaster was privy to the answers to the questions. The situational factors were largely ignored in favour of attributing the participant's lack of success to something about them, that being the assumed intelligence of the participant.

5.4.4.2.2 JUST WORLD BIAS: INJUSTICE EXPERIMENTS

Learner and Simmons (1986) observed a curious phenomenon amongst healthcare professionals, who, though otherwise balanced and caring, on occasion, blamed patients for their ailments. Learner and Simmons used Stanley Milgram's obedience experiment as a mechanism with which to explore this in more detail. Observers were instructed to watch a subject solve a problem, if the problem was not solved the subject appeared to receive a painful electric shock (in reality, there was no electric shock and the subject was a stooge working in concert with the researchers). Typically, the observers devalued and brought into question the character of those that failed to solve the problem and, subsequently, received an electronic shock. As such, the observers constructed a reality to justify why the subjects received an electric shock.

5.4.4.2.3 AVAILABILITY BIAS: KNIFE CRIME IN BRITAIN

The availability bias helps us make speedy judgements, although it leads to errors. For instance, in 2018 there was a spate of knife crimes in London and the media coverage was predictably sensational, The Sun's headline read 'Mummy died saving my life'. 'Daughter's heart-breaking dance tribute to hero mum, 43, who died in her arms after being knifed saving her in Christmas party brawl', and the Daily Express asked, 'How many more innocents must die?' Whilst the suggestion is that there was an upsurge in knife crime, the sad reality is that knife crime has been a problem in Britain for many years and for those living in these affected communities this is not new news, yet those outside these communities make judgements based on media coverage and assume there has been an explosion in knife crime.

5.4.4.2.4 BEAUTY IS GOOD BIAS: ATTRACTIVENESS AND EMPLOYMENT

Even in more liberal times, an attractiveness bias can be still found in the workplace. Those that are deemed physically attractive are more likely to be interviewed, hired and are less likely to be sacked. Attractiveness is largely based on pervading stereotypes of what constitutes aesthetically pleasing. Inevitably, the beauty bias discriminates against those who do not conform to the normative expectations about appearance. As such, tattoos, piercings, unusual clothing and even being overweight can result in unjust judgements not just in the workplace but in general.

5.4.4.2.5 IN-GROUP AND OUT-GROUP BIAS: SOCIALLY DESIRABLE BEHAVIOUR

Taylor and Jaggi (1974) were interested in how we make in-group and out-group judgements. The researchers conducted a study in southern India where they instructed Hindu participants to read paragraphs describing socially desirable or undesirable behaviour performed by the in-group (Hindu) or out-group (Muslim) members. Participants were asked to state whether the behaviour was a product of dispositional or situational factors. Participants gave contrasting attributions to socially desirable behaviour, based on whether the observed subject was a Hindu or a Muslim.

■ If the subject was a Hindu, then the socially desirable behaviour was attributed to dispositional factors.
■ When the subject was a Muslim, then socially desirable behaviour was attributed to situational factors.

It would seem that when considering socially desirable behaviour, we are more likely to make dispositional attributions for the group we identify with and make situational attributions for the group we do not identify with.

5.4.4.3 *Cultural differences and judgement bias*

It was first thought that the fundamental attribution error was a universal phenomenon. However, it has been proven that individualistic societies, often found in western cultures, place a considerably greater emphasis on dispositional attributes than more collective cultures.

5.4.4.3.1 JAPANESE VERSUS AMERICAN CULTURES

In a study conducted by Masuda and Nisbett (2001), Japanese and American students were presented with a picture of brightly coloured fish swimming in the foreground with vegetation in the background. All were asked to mention what they recalled about the picture. Whilst all students mentioned the brightly coloured fish swimming in the foreground, the Japanese students were much more likely to mention detail in the background, including vegetation and a frog. In other words, the Japanese students included situational aspects of the picture that were largely ignored by the American students.

5.4.4.3.2 INDIAN VERSUS AMERICAN CULTURES

Miller (1984) looked at adult and children's attribution in India and America. There were three subject groups, children aged 8–11 years, teenagers aged 15 years and adults. Each group was asked to account for several pro- and antisocial behaviours. Miller observed that there was little difference in attribution between the two cultures for children aged 8 to 11 years. For older children and adults, there was a difference. Reflecting a more individualistic culture, older Americans made more dispositional attributions about the behaviour they were asked to account for, than those from India. It seems a more collective society results in more situational attributions of the same behaviour.

5.4.4.3.3 BICULTURAL VALUES

Hong et al. (2000) looked at attribution bias amongst high school students in Hong Kong, where traditional Chinese values are taught but where over 100 years of English territorial rule has resulted in a blend of English and Chinese values. The students were randomly assigned to one of the three priming conditions:

■ Those in the American culture condition saw pictures of American icons, such as, the Capitol Building and American Flag and were then asked to write down a few sentences about American culture.
■ Those in the Chinese culture condition saw pictures of Chinese icons, such as, a Chinese Dragon and the Great Wall of China and were then asked to write a few sentences about Chinese culture.
■ Those in the control condition saw pictures of landscapes and were then asked to write down a few sentences about those landscapes.

A story about an overweight boy was then shared with all the students: the boy had been advised by a doctor not to eat food with high sugar content; nonetheless, he was at a buffet and had eaten a cake. The students were then asked to indicate the extent to which the boy's weight problem was a product of dispositional or situational factors. Those that were primed with the American iconography were more likely to attribute behaviour to disposition as compared to those that were primed by Chinese iconography. Attribution from those in the control condition fell somewhere between the American and Chinese culture conditioning cohorts.

5.4.5 How to guard against judgement bias

There are several things researchers can do to reduce the impact of bias on their research, as detailed in Figure 5.14.

Be mindful of possible attribution bias

- Although it might seem obvious, simply being mindful of the various attribution biases can help reduce the likelihood of bias creeping into research.
- On a cautionary note, it is impossible to eradicate bias in entirety.

Consensus check the questions you want to ask

- Bias can occur in regard to what questions are asked and how they are asked.
- Prior to conducting any research, consensus check your questions to spot any possible bias.

Look at the world through the participant's lens

- Be mindful that whilst we are the observers, we need to look at the world through the lens of the participant.

Consider the bigger picture

- Draw upon any contextual information that might be available.
- Review all the available signals, both verbal and nonverbal, remember, 70% of all communication is nonverbal.

Challenge your initial assumptions

- Analysis is an iterative process, develop counter narratives to test and challenge your initial thinking.
- Analysis is a shared endeavour, defer to others when trying to make sense of the participant narrative.

Figure 5.14 Reducing bias in research

5.4.6 Implications for behavioural research

1 Biases exhibited by participants should not be dismissed out of hand. Yes, they result in attribution errors, but they are also a reflection of a participant's opinion of themselves and others.

2 A key bias is fundamental attribution error, where we tend to attribute other people's behaviour to dispositional factors at the expense of considering the influence of situational factors. This type of bias can lead to stereotyping and prejudice.

3 As researchers, we are equally prone to bias that does make the job of making sense of participant behaviour somewhat challenging, although the techniques discussed in this chapter will help to guard against attribution bias.

5.4.7 References/further reading

Bauman, K. P., and Geher, G. (2002). We Think You Agree: The Detrimental Impact of the False Consensus Effect on Behavior. *Current Psychology*, 21 (4), pp. 293–318.

Hong, Y.-y., Morris, M. W., Chiu, C.-y., and Benet-Martínez, V. (2000). Multicultural Minds: A Dynamic Constructivist Approach to Culture and Cognition. *American Psychologist*, 55 (7), pp. 709–720.

Lerner, M. J., and Simmons, C. H. (1966). Observer's Reaction to the "Innocent Victim": Compassion or Rejection? *Journal of Personality and Social Psychology*, 4 (2), pp. 203–210.

Masuda, T., and Nisbett, R. E. (2001). Attending Holistically Versus Analytically: Comparing the Context Sensitivity of Japanese and Americans. *Journal of Personality and Social Psychology*, 81 (5), pp. 922–934.

Miller, J. G. (1984). Culture and the Development of Everyday Social Explanation. *Journal of Personality and Social Psychology*, 46 (5), pp. 961–978.

Sedikides, C., Campbell, W. K., Reeder, G. D., and Elliot, A. J. (1998). The Self-Serving Bias in Relational Context. *Journal of Personality and Social Psychology*, 74 (2), pp. 378–386.

Skitka, L. J., Mullen, E., Griffin, T., Hutchinson, S., and Chamberlin, B. (2002). Dispositions, Scripts, or Motivated Correction? Understanding Ideological Differences in Explanations for Social Problems. *Journal of Personality and Social Psychology*, 83 (2), pp. 470–487.

Taylor, D. M., and Jaggi, V. (1974). Ethnocentrism and Causal Attribution in a South Indian Context. *Journal of Cross-Cultural Psychology*, 5 (2), pp. 162–171.

The newspaper articles mentioned can be found at:

Carter, H. (2018). Mummy Died Saving My Life, Daughter's Heart-Breaking Dance Tribute to Hero Mum, 43, Who Died in Her Arms after Being Knifed Saving Her in Christmas Party Brawl. *The Sun*, 30th December. https://www.thesun.co.uk/news/8087147/daughters-dance-tribute-to-mum-stabbed-at-christmas/ [accessed 03/05/2021].

Dixon, C., and Twomey, J. (2018). How Many More Innocents Must Die? *Daily Express*, 4th April. https://www.pressreader.com/uk/daily-express/20180404/281487866912416 [accessed 03/05/2021].

5.4.7.1 Want to know more?

Friedrich Försterling's book provides a good overview of the bias discussed in this chapter.

Försterling, F. (2001). *Attribution: An Introduction to Theories, Research and Applications*. East Sussex: Psychology Press Ltd.

Chapter 6

How to select theory

CHAPTER OVERVIEW

6.1 We begin by addressing the challenges facing researchers in selecting theory.

6.2 Next, the key steps to theory selection are discussed.

6.3 Finally, closing arguments about the role theory plays in behavioural research are presented.

Introduction

In this book, we have looked at different theories and considered their application within the field of market research. In the opening chapter, we discussed the importance of considering theory that addresses both social structure and individual agency when looking to explain human behaviour. Perhaps understandably, it can be difficult to know which theory or theories to use, under what circumstances and how best to apply theory in practice. In this final chapter, we address these issues and propose a five-step guide to theory selection.

6.1 The underuse, selective use and misuse of theory

We can attest to the sheer scale of theory in social science, drawn from different schools of thought, subscribing to different research philosophies, resulting

DOI: 10.4324/9781003169932-6

in a disparate and fragmented body of knowledge. There have been attempts at theory synthesis, although mostly with limited success; a key drawback is that unifying theory limits critical reflection and generalisability to the social world. Moreover, theory is largely written by academics for academics, often using obscure language that is alien to the uninitiated. As such, theory is often seen as nonsensical and inaccessible to the layperson. Unfortunately, this can result in theory being avoided, applied selectively or misused. There is no magic bullet to this problem; however, it is hoped that the five-step guide discussed in this chapter will provide researchers with a logical and structured approach to selecting theory.

6.2 Key stages to theory selection

6.2.1 Defining the research problem, a precursor to theory selection

Prior to considering theory selection, it will be important to spend time thinking about and exploring the research problem. Defining the research problem should communicate the vision and scope of the research which will help ensure its success. Moreover, defining the research problem will help ensure that only theory that is pursuant to the research problem is considered.

Typically, research addresses either a theoretical problem that exists in academia or a practical problem that addresses a need, although on occasion research addresses both.

- A theoretical problem might be a gap in academic knowledge that you have spotted or has been lighted upon by researchers in that field.
- A practical problem might be based on personal experience or an issue that you have observed impacting a group or wider society.

Mostly, in market research, research is commissioned to address a practical problem, albeit there is a progressive move in academia towards addressing more practical problems. A practical problem might be understanding the needs of a target audience, testing a new product, reviewing marketing executions and so on.

6.2.2 Selecting theory

Theory selection should start broad and through a process of theory 'stress testing', the selection is narrowed down to a single or select few theories that are thought to

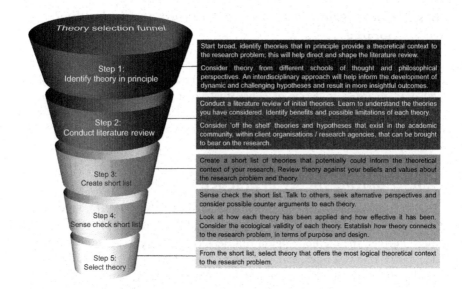

Figure 6.1 entries:

Step 1:
Identify theory in principle

Start broad, identify theories that in principle provide a theoretical context to the research problem; this will help direct and shape the literature review.

Consider theory from different schools of thought and philosophical perspectives. An interdisciplinary approach will help inform the development of dynamic and challenging hypotheses and result in more insightful outcomes.

Step 2:
Conduct literature review

Conduct a literature review of initial theories. Learn to understand the theories you have considered. Identify benefits and possible limitations of each theory.

Consider 'off the shelf' theories and hypotheses that exist in the academic community, within client organisations / research agencies, that can be brought to bear on the research.

Step 3:
Create short list

Create a short list of theories that potentially could inform the theoretical context of your research. Review theory against your beliefs and values about the research problem and theory.

Sense check the short list. Talk to others, seek alternative perspectives and consider possible counter arguments to each theory.

Step 4:
Sense check short list

Look at how each theory has been applied and how effective it has been. Consider the ecological validity of each theory. Establish how theory connects to the research problem, in terms of purpose and design.

Step 5:
Select theory

From the short list, select theory that offers the most logical theoretical context to the research problem.

Figure 6.1 Theory selection funnel

offer the best theoretical backdrop to the research problem. In Figure 6.1, a theory selection funnel is presented detailing the key stages of this process.

It is hoped that by using the above theory selection funnel, researchers will consider theory, not as an afterthought but embrace theory as a key decision tool in the process of conducting research.

6.3 Conclusion: applying theory in behavioural research

6.3.1 Theory as a research decision tool

This book has unequivocally addressed the nature and purpose of theory in behavioural research. Presenting theory as a research decision tool helps illustrate how theory influences all facets of the research process, from initially connecting researchers to a body of knowledge to informing the implementation of research outcomes. It is hoped that in presenting theory in an accessible and intelligible manner its role in providing causal explanations for human behaviour has been clearly demonstrated.

6.3.2 Considering both social structure and individual agency

The interplay between social structure and individual agency suggests that researchers should be cognisant of both theoretical perspectives. Inevitably, this will lead to issues in terms of conceptual inconsistencies from one theory to another. That said, the benefits of developing a richer theoretical context in which to view research far outweigh the possible shortcomings of dealing with conceptual inconsistencies.

6.3.3 Applying theory in practice

The practical examples of applying theory detailed throughout this book help to dispel the commonly held belief that theory is difficult to apply to real-world settings. Further, the methodological tips detailed throughout are intended to help demonstrate how to operationalise theory. As we have seen, theories vary significantly, some are more parsimonious than others, some are easier to comprehend than others, some are more generalisable than others and some are more testable than others. Against this backdrop, it is acknowledged that selecting theory is challenging, which can deter researchers from using theory, or result in theory being applied only selectively or even incorrectly. The theory selection funnel detailed in this final chapter will help provide researchers with clear guidance on theory selection.

6.3.4 And finally

It is hoped that having read this book, the reader will come away with a fuller appreciation of the role of theory and be inspired to seek out and explore theory in greater detail, whether it be within the discipline of market research or more generally in seeking causal explanations for human behaviour in everyday life.

Index

Note: **Bold** page numbers refer to tables; *italic* page numbers refer to figures.

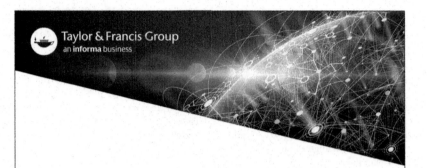